THE AUSTRALIAN
CHRISTMAS BOOK

THE AUSTRALIAN
CHRISTMAS BOOK

KAY FAIRFAX

Angus&Robertson

An imprint of HarperCollinsPublishers

An Angus & Robertson Publication

Angus&Robertson, an imprint of
HarperCollins*Publishers*
25 Ryde Road, Pymble, Sydney NSW 2073, Australia
31 View Road, Glenfield, Auckland 10, New Zealand
77–85 Fulham Palace Road, London W6 8JB, United Kingdom
10 East 53rd Street, New York NY 10022, USA

First published in Australia in 1994
Copyright © Kay Fairfax 1994

National Library of Australia
Cataloguing-in-Publication data:

Fairfax, Kay.
    The Australian Christmas Book.
    ISBN 0 207 18410 0.
    1. Christmas decorations – Australia. 2. Christmas cookery.
    3. Cookery, Australian. 4. Handicraft. I. Title.
745.59412

Photography by Andrew Elton
Illustrations by Dianne Bradley
Design by Darian Causby and Kerry Klinner
Printed by Griffin Press in Australia

9 8 7 6 5 4 3 2 1
97 96 95 94

ACKNOWLEDGMENTS

Many people have helped in the compilation of this book.
I would like to make a special mention of my daughter, Dimity Fairfax and Pam Cooper for their help,
and of Andrew Elton, whose photography has lifted this book from the ordinary to the extraordinary,
and of my Publisher, Alison Pressley, without whose help and support there would be no book.

I would also like to thank the following people: Justine Mainwaring,
Fruzsina Mainwaring, Nigel Mainwaring, Helen Palk, Cameron Palk, Cindy Fairfax, Duncan and
Jacqui Fairfax, Katie Locke, Janet Payne, John Payne, Bruce Rosenberg, Helen Rowe, Kate Russell,
Sally Heath of Abba Interiors, Lisa Heath, John Heath, Pam Cooper, Jane Allen, James and
Stacey Dunlop, Dennis Brown, Annie Vinter, Jon Wilson, Keith Adams, Chris Jacovides, Susie Elder,
Beverly Brown, Jill Hamilton, Victoria Drew, Louisa Drew, Gina Taranto, Rosie Taranto, Jack Taranto,
Ros Innes of Melahdine Handcrafts (Berrima, NSW), David Scarlett of Scarletts (Burrawang, NSW),
Maryann and Simon Rasmussen of Bourke Street Cellars (Darlinghurst, NSW), Kevin Watson,
John and Betty Hunt, Catherine Lightfoot, the staff of The Blue Cockerel (Mittagong, NSW) and
Roger Brown of Roger Brown Wine Agencies (82 Grosvenor Street, Wahroonga, NSW 2076) for his
wonderful suggestions for Australian wines to accompany the meals.

I also thank Debbie Conna of Homecraft Stores for supplying me,
free of charge, with all the materials and goods for the craft items. Homecraft is Australia's largest
craft store with every craft imaginable, from home decorating to jewellery making, textiles and
needlework to candlewicking, basketry to pickling and much more. At the time of going to press,
certain specialised craft items such as the 'Crystal Reflections' tree decoration kits are exclusive to
Homecraft Stores, although it may be possible to buy similar versions elsewhere. If you wish to make
any of the crafts described in *The Australian Christmas Book*, you are sure to find all the resources you
need at Homecraft. You might even want to join one of their classes or workshops and learn new skills,
or get the children involved. Homecraft is open seven days a week; contact them on (02) 647 1122 and
ask for a free newsletter.

I also thank the following people for generously allowing their poetry to appear in this book: Dr John
Bray, for *Xmas 1961*; Jeff Guess for *Melaleuca Morning*; Rhyll McMaster for *A Festive Poem*; and Myron
Lysenko for *Christmas Holidays*. The wood engravings which appear on pages 12–13, 44–45, 80–81,
109, 121, 133 and 173 are courtesy of the La Trobe Collection, State Library of Victoria. The lyrics of
Carol of the Birds by John Harry Rupert Wheeler and William Garnet James appear couresty of
Chappell & Co. Australia.

CONTENTS

FESTIVE FOOD 80

INDEX 174

INTRODUCTION

Although many of our Christmas traditions stem from Europe, we are now a multicultural nation with access to many different customs and foods from all parts of the world. No matter where we come from we have to accept new traditions and adapt old ones to the Australian climate! This is the greatest factor affecting what we eat at Christmas and what we call a traditional Christmas.

Australia is emerging with a unique cuisine that is a mixture of British, European and Asian influences. In this book you will find many new recipes and decorative ideas which utilise the incredible variety of Australian plants and food that are in season during our summer Christmas.

I have tried to emphasize the simple joys of Christmas, the small pleasures that we can so easily overlook in our hectic lifestyles with ever-present pressures that can make it practically impossible to relax and enjoy this time of year. My aim is to make the preparation of Christmas festivities as much fun as the festivities themselves. With a little planning and patience, you can recapture the true spirit of Christmas and enjoy this special time of the year with the people you love.

Try and make time to share the preparations with children and grandparents, whether it means cooking together, making decorations or wrapping gifts. Times like these are what memories are made of, and it is also how family traditions begin. Whatever you are creating, when you share the process with someone else, it somehow makes it more special. It is also much more exciting for the children to feel they are involved with the preparations – and it helps to keep their hands busy and channel their energy into something constructive!

As Henry Wadsworth Longfellow said:

'The heart hath its own memory, like the mind
And in it are enshrined
The precious keepsakes, into which is wrought
The giver's loving thought.'

Choosing which poems would be included in this book has been a very interesting experience. Time and time again our irreverent Australian sense of humour has been evident! I particularly like this cryptic verse, written by John Bray:

XMAS 1961
Hark, the store directors sing,
Listen to the till-bells ring,
Credit free and waste run wild,
Holt and Holdens reconciled,
Piles of trash and tinsel rise,
Potted carols rend the skies,
Christ we hail with glad applause,
Born to sponsor Santa Claus.
Hark, the store directors sing,
Listen to the till-bells ring.

Written over thirty years ago, this poem is still relevant today! Hopefully, though, we will continue to move away from such commercialisation to a simpler and more spiritually oriented Christmas.

This book includes activities for all the family – presents to make, gift wrapping ideas, decorations and, of course, the preparation and presentation of festive food. I have concentrated on recipes that can be prepared well ahead of time, thus helping to keep you out of the kitchen on a hot Christmas Day day!

Despite the fact that Christmas falls in the middle of summer we can – with a little planning – make our celebrations as beautiful and exciting as those anywhere else in the world, without losing the atmosphere and meaning of this special time of the year. So, let your creative expression have a free rein and, as the old saying goes, 'Eat, drink and be merry!'

KAY FAIRFAX

DECORATIONS

THE CHRISTMAS
Tree

I n Australia we tend to associate the traditional evergreen trees of Europe with Christmas. In this chapter are some different ideas you may like to try, including edible Christmas trees and Christmas trees made from materials readily available in Australia. There are also ideas for Christmas tree decorations that are simple to make and can be custom made to suit your own tastes.

CHRISTMAS TREES

In 1500, the Christmas tree was the centre of outdoor celebrations in Central European countries such as Estonia and Latvia. There, the villagers would place an evergreen tree in the main square and dance around it, finally setting it alight.

The Germans were the first to bring the Christmas tree indoors. As a symbol of Adam and Eve and their expulsion from Paradise, they decorated their trees with shiny red apples. Until the advent of electricity at the beginning of the 19th century, real candles were always used to light the tree.

Christmas trees were introduced to Great Britain in the 1840s by Queen Charlotte, the wife of King George III. This custom was continued by the German-born Prince Albert, who decorated the first tree at Windsor Castle with ornaments from his native Germany. From this time on, trees really became the focal point of Christmas celebrations in English homes, and the custom was soon adopted in America and Australia. The first electrically lit tree appeared in New York in 1882.

For many years, Christmas trees were decorated with foods such as apples, marzipan fruits, biscuits, nuts, large raisins and any fruits in season. The tradition developed that these decorations could not be eaten until 6 January, then the children of the house were allowed to shake the tree and eat all they could catch.

> *All topiary trees are made in the same way, whether you use a base bought from a craft shop or make your own. Just about anything can be used, from fresh flowers to lollipops, sweets, dried flowers, holly, fruit and paper.*

PREVIOUS PAGES: *Examples of the types of trees you can make using homemade bases or readymade styrofoam balls (second from the left) and wooden stick tree bases (used for trees first and fifth from the left).*

CHRISTMAS TREE SKIRT

Cut a circle of felt, or any heavy Christmas-coloured fabric large enough to fit around the tree base and to spread out on the floor.

Mark the centre of the circle of fabric and cut from the centre point to one edge. Cut a smaller circle in the middle, just large enough to fit around the trunk of the tree. Sew or glue binding around the centre circle, along the open edges and all around the outside circle. Sew a length of matching coloured tape on either side of the small circle to tie the skirt in place. Glue on small contrasting felt shapes to decorate the skirt.

TOPIARY TREES

wooden dowel, cut to the required length
green paint or green florist's tape
1 garden pot
ready-mixed cement or Polyfilla
styrofoam ball or pyramid, or Oasis if using real flowers
gravel or wood chips
shallow funnel
florist's clay

Cut one end of the dowel to a point and paint it, or cover it with florist's tape. To achieve a more realistic effect, a straight tree branch is ideal — a broom handle will do.

Fill the pot with cement or Polyfilla. (A small pot can be filled with Polyfilla, but because this is so expensive, when filling a large pot, use ready-mixed cement.) Secure the dowel, with the sharpened end uppermost. Position the styrofoam ball or pyramid over the point and press. Cover the cement with gravel or woodchips.

If you are using fresh flowers, you will need a shallow funnel and florist's clay to secure the oasis to the funnel. Completely saturate the oasis and fit it into the funnel. (The best way to achieve a balanced effect between the pot and the top section is to make the finished size of the top section approximately the same size as the diameter of the top of the pot.)

GRAPE VINE TREE

chicken wire
grape vine cuttings
ribbon bows or fairy lights (optional)

Construct a frame of chicken wire in the shape and size you require, it can be cone shaped, branched or pyramidal. Weave the vines around the frame until the wire is completely covered. Decorate with small bows, fairy lights or any decorations you like. These bases are great for making small trees as centrepieces for your Christmas-table setting.

IVY TREE

pot of choice
potting mix
ivy (Pittsburg or Californian ivy are both ideal, as they branch naturally and will survive being cut back. English ivy is less suitable as it has larger leaves and tends to trail)
strong wire
fine wire

Fill the pot with potting mix and plant the ivy.

🐾 Use the strong wire to make the frame (wire coathangers are ideal) and the finer wire to join the sections. (Ready-made frames are available from most nurseries, but by making your own you can ensure it is exactly the right size to fit your pot.) Train the ivy to wind around the frame and do not allow it to grow vertically.

🐾 If you wish to expand the shape of your tree, add extra lengths of heavy wire and train the ivy to cover it.

🐾 When constructing the frame, make sure its base fits well down into the pot.

🐾 The length of wire used for the frame will depend on your choice of pot and the size you wish to make the frame. As a guide, take three even lengths of heavy wire and bind them together at the top with the fine wire. When secure, shape the heavy wire out to fit the pot.

Choosing a traditional Christmas tree

The first thing to check when buying your tree is that it has been recently cut. When you get it home, plunge it immediately into a bucket of cold water. Then prepare your stand or bucket. You can now buy special Christmas tree stands which also have water trays to fit any size tree trunk. The most important thing to remember is that the tree needs water, and it should not be placed in solid dirt. If you are improvising at home, it is preferable to use pebbles or stones in a container to prop up the tree. Make sure there is plenty of water in the container to begin with and remember to top it up. Your tree should then last for at least twelve days.

POPCORN TREE

1 egg white
2½ cups (6 oz/185 g) icing sugar, sifted
1½ tablespoons water
5–6 drops green food colouring
6 large ice-cream cones
3 cups (6 oz/180 g) popcorn, allowing ½ cup (1 oz/30 g) for each tree
small red sweets or red marzipan balls

Mix the egg white, icing sugar and water to make a paste. Gradually add the green food colouring. Cover the ice-cream cones with the paste. Press the popcorn into the paste to cover each cone and decorate with red sweets. (You can use any lolly you like to decorate these trees.)

🐾 These trees are great for kids — they can take one home with them after the Christmas party.

🐾 Use the same basic method to make a large popcorn tree — use a polystyrene shape instead of ice-cream cones. Or you could even use an edible base moulded into the required shape.

Makes 6 trees.

CHOCOLATE CRACKLE TREE

Chocolate crackles

4 cups (250 g/8 oz) Rice Bubbles

⅔ cup (90 g/3 oz) cocoa

1 ½ cups (185 g/6 oz) icing sugar, sifted

1 cup (125 g/4 oz) desiccated coconut

250 g (8 oz) copha, melted

2–3 drops vanilla essence

Tree

1 polystyrene cone

aluminium foil

1 egg white

2 cups (250 g/8 oz) icing sugar, sifted

½ cup (60 g/2 oz) cocoa

1 ½ tablespoons water

red and green marzipan, for decoration

Make the chocolate crackles: combine the Rice Bubbles, cocoa, icing sugar and coconut. Add the melted copha and vanilla essence to the dry mixture and mix well. Shape into rounded tablespoon-sized balls and cool. Makes about 36.

Make the tree: wrap the cone completely with the aluminium foil. Mix the egg white, icing sugar, cocoa and water to make a thick icing mixture. Cover the cone with three-quarters of the mixture. Start building the tree from the bottom, sticking each crackle on with a little of the extra icing. Add a few green leaves and red berries made from marzipan.

RIGHT: *This Father Christmas tree is made using the readymade styrofoam pyramid base pictured beside it. Father Christmas is made from wood shavings, calico, buttons and glasses.*
BELOW: *Crystal reflections (page 25).*

RED FELT POINSETTIAS

red felt
thin hat elastic
large darning needle
8 small wooden beads

Cut eight red felt leaves as shown in the illustration below. Fold the bottom tip of each leaf in the middle and thread the elastic through, then thread a bead. Continue threading with the remaining leaves and beads alternately until completed. Tie the elastic off in a knot.

Red felt poinsettias look pretty hanging on the tree or arranged with holly down the middle of the table. They also make attractive decorations for parcels and on jars containing Christmas jams or preserves.

CHRISTMAS BELLS

coloured cardboard or felt
pencil
stapler
staples
needle
matching cotton thread
spray adhesive (optional)
fabric with small Christmas pattern (optional)

Cut three large or small pieces of cardboard or felt as per the pattern below. Place the three layers on top of each other. Mark the middle of the bell with a pencil line, staple lengthwise at the top and bottom of the line, then put one or two more staples evenly along the rest of the line. Fold out the six sections to form the bell.

Using doubled matching thread, stitch through the top of the bell and then pass the needle back through the middle of the double thread. Cut the threads and tie off to the required length for hanging.

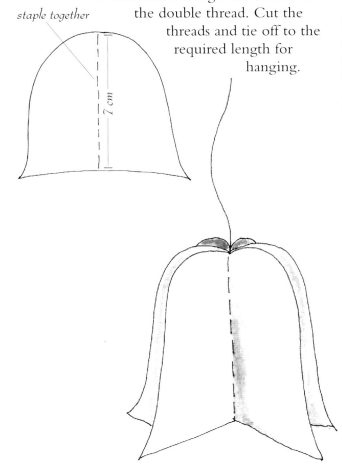

staple together

7 cm

MINI-GARDEN-POT BELLS

These are made from very small terracotta pots, turned upside down, decorated on the top and threaded with a ribbon for hanging. Make sure the knot inside the top of the pot is large enough not to pull through the hole. You can also attach a small bell to the inside of the pot by tying it around the ribbon knot.

CRYSTAL REFLECTIONS

These clear plastic shapes are available in stars, balls, santas, teardrops, hearts and bells.

🌼 Trim them with ribbons, lace, beads or dried flowers — all can be attached to the top of the shape with craft wire.

🌼 Or decorate using fabric paints on the outside of the shapes with a variety of designs. Or fill the inside of the shapes with miniature collectables. Or fill them with lollies or a special gift.

PLAITED PAPER CONE BASKETS

Cut two patterns as per the diagram below in contrasting coloured paper (one of each colour). Fold each pattern in half with the right sides to the outside. Cut through the marked lines, making sure both sections are exactly even, or the cone will not work properly. (Make sure the cutting lines are even and that they run parallel to the outer edge of the cone.) Hold the two rounded ends between the thumb and index finger of each hand.

fold line

cut
cut
cut

🌼 Thread the first strip (double) held in the right hand through the middle of the first strip held in the left hand. Now thread the doubled second strip of the left section through the middle of the first right hand strip. This part must be done correctly for it to be a success. Continue to thread the first right through the third left, then the fourth left through the first right.

🌼 Continue to plait the remaining strips in the same manner until the basket is completed. Gently pull both sections to tighten the weaving.

🌼 For the handle: cut a narrow strip of either coloured paper to the required length and glue it into position to the inside of opposite sides of the basket.

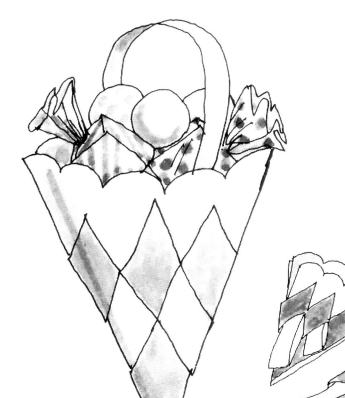

25

FROM THE Garden

Plants can be used to make all
sorts of fresh and imaginative
Christmas decorations and
ornaments. This chapter includes
instructions and inspiration on how to
make traditional things such as
evergreen garlands and wreaths, swags
and pomanders — as well as giving
you ideas on using native-plant flowers,
leaves, seeds and pods. The emphasis is
on simple and easy-to-make ideas that
can be created with materials from your
own garden.

FESTIVE GARLANDS

The easiest way to make a garland is to place, in a garden or flour sieve, the clippings or twigs to be used. Flour sieves come in many sizes and are ideal for making smaller garlands as they ensure a circular shape.

To make a heavy based garland in winter, cut the new growth from willow, apple, pear or plum trees and place them in a circular container roughly 45 cm (18 in) across. Leave them to dry.

For a very easy garland, save the late-autumn cuttings taken from grape, wisteria and clematis vines. Wind at least three circles together and hold them in place with wire. Hang in a well-aired place until ready to use. Once dried, they can be painted white, gold or silver, or given a coat of clear gloss, depending on the look you want to achieve.

For a traditional Scandinavian garland, plan ahead and collect fine birch twigs in autumn and winter. Select the longest and the finest twigs, twist them until they overlap each other and tie them in four places with string. To make a more informal garland, use hay or wheat instead or birch twigs.

Once the garland base is made you can add many different decorations — dried leaves, flowers, pine cones, seed pods, fresh or dried herbs, red sweet peppers (capsicums) or chillies, bows, small parcels, fruits or marzipan fruits. Carefully wire all decorations in place and finish with a large Christmas bow to match.

For the birch and hay garlands, evenly wind stiffened Christmas ribbon (see page 76) around the garland and trim it with a large bow of matching ribbon.

Miniature garlands can be made from wheat, oat or barley straws plaited into a circle and trimmed with a ribbon or matching bow.

Remember to wire a hook at the top of your garland for hanging.

PREVIOUS PAGES: *Nest made of wheat (page 40), decorated with Christmas eggs (page 76).*

FLOWER BALLS

For a full-circle ball:
2 wire-framed baskets
strong wire
water retentive moss
light potting mix
compact seedlings of your choice
wire or rope, for hanging

For a half-circle ball:
1 wire-framed basket
fibre planter lining
light potting mix
sharp knife
compact seedlings of your choice
wire or rope, for hanging

To make a full-circle flower ball, wire the two baskets together. Line the ball frame with water-retentive moss and fill with light potting mix. Make a small cup-like indentation at the top of the frame lining to help store water. Poke holes through the wire and moss, making sure you dig deeply enough to reach the soil. Plant the compact seedlings about 16 cm (6 in) apart all around the frame.

If you are using only one basket to make a half-circle flower ball, line it with fibre and fill it with light potting mix. You will need a sharp knife to make slits through the fibre. Plant about four seedlings in the top of the basket, spacing them evenly. Continue planting seedlings all around the outside of the basket, about 10 cm (4 in) apart.

Once the plants in your flower ball have established themselves, keep picking any spent blooms to encourage new buds. For the best results, water the flower ball daily and apply a little liquid fertiliser about twice a month. Hang the basket in a sunny position.

For summer planting in most parts of Australia, choose hardy plants like petunias, impatiens, lobelias and begonias are ideal. Also, miniature chrysanthemums look wonderful and, for an absolutely spectacular effect, choose miniature poinsettias.

EVERGREEN WREATHS

greenery
wire, cane or grape vine to make the frame (or buy a
   readymade frame)
tightly packed moss or straw, for base
decorations
Christmas ribbon

Wreaths can be made from many different types
of evergreen — fir, holly, ivy, bay, laurel, box and
even herbs like thyme are suitable.

The frame for an evergreen wreath is usually
made from wire, cane or grape vine. Readymade
frames can be purchased from most craft shops.
Alternatively, they can be made by wiring two or
three lengths of strong wire together (coathangers
are ideal). Wind the wire around a garden or flour
sieve to ensure the wreath frame is circular.

A good base for a wreath is tightly packed
moss or straw, which can be dampened to help
the foliage stay fresh longer. The finished wreath
should be 4–5 cm (1½–2 in) thick.

Cut each piece of greenery about 9 cm
(3½ in) long, steep the ends in water and spray the
foliage with water. If the wreath is to be used on
a door or a table it need not be covered at the
back. Arrange the pieces of greenery in the same
direction, so that they fit closely together and
overlap slightly. Evenly wire the greenery into
place with florist's wire or green string.

Finally, trim the wreath with Christmas
ribbon, and finish with a large matching bow.

Ideas for decorating evergreen wreaths and garlands

*Have your wreath decorations ready and
wired together in clusters. Many decorations
may be purchased already wired, but if you
are using marzipan or real fruits you will need
to wire them yourself. This is done by
threading a fine wire through the bottom end of
each piece of fruit or nut, and then twisting the
wire ends together, leaving enough wire to
secure it to the garland.*

*Glue small nuts and cones together and then
wire them, again twisting the ends and leaving
one end long enough to secure the cluster onto
the wreath. Some of the larger nuts and pods
may need to have holes burnt through their
shells with a hot skewer before the wire may
be threaded through.*

*Try using short fat candles as decorations for
a table wreath; be careful, however, to wire
them on securely so they do not come in contact
with any of the greenery.*

NUT, CONE AND SEED POD WREATH

variety of nuts, cones and seed pods
glue gun
3 ply board, cut to a circle, size as required
clear or lightly coloured gloss paint

If necessary for successful gluing, sand the decorations to flatten the surface; some may need to be cut in half. Using the glue gun as directed, glue the nuts, cones and seed pods on the board.

Fill the spaces with little nuts or seed pods so no gaps show from above or the sides. Allow the glue to dry. To cover the glue, paint with two coats of paint. Drill a hole in the top and insert a circle of wire for hanging. Finish off the wreath with ribbons and bows.

RIGHT: *Wreath (page 37) made with a grape vine base and decorated with evergreens and a variety of seed pods and nuts.*
BELOW: *Vine nest (page 40) made from clematis and birch twigs. The decorations include pine cones, gum leaves and dried flowers.*

NESTS

vines of your choice such as bean and grape or dried
  wheat
nylon thread
grasses, wheat, oats, barley, nuts, feathers, insects,
  leaves, dried flowers, ribbon or ornamental birds for
  lining and decoration

Twist the vines or wheat into a nest shape and
secure them with nylon thread. Tuck the lining
and/or decorations into the nesting material, in
much the same manner as a real bird's nest.

RED APPLE SWAG

This is a very simple idea that takes minutes to
make but can give the home the added touch of
festivity you are after at Christmas time.

Choose small, bright red apples of equal size,
or a variety of colours. Wash, dry and polish
them. Place the apples on a large sheet of clear
cellophane paper in a line, leaving enough space
between each apple to twist the paper several
times. Tie a narrow ribbon bow around each
twist and a loop and bow at each end. You can
also add bows at each twist of the swag.

Ideas for decorating nests

Collect hen, duck, goose, quail or turkey eggs to
place in the nest. Make a tiny hole in both ends
and blow out the contents. Rinse the eggs in
water and then again with diluted bleach to
preserve them. Decorate the eggs with a
Christmas theme.
  Alternatively, a nest from grape vine cuttings
makes an attractive decoration at Christmas
time when filled with sweets. (When the festive
season is over it can be used in the kitchen as
an egg basket.) Choose festive sweets, such as
sugar coated almonds, gold foil-covered
chocolate coins or chocolate-covered nuts.

Swags

Swags look wonderful along the mantlepiece,
around the fireplace or doorway, up the
staircase or looped around the table —
anywhere you want to add a bit of colour and
interest. For greenery swags, you will need
strong green rope, secateurs, gardening gloves
and strong green string. Measure the amount
of rope you will need and loop and drape it as
you want. Cut the evergreen in lengths of about
25 cm (10 in) and, using five or six pieces at a
time, bind them onto the rope with string,
making sure the foliage lays in the one
direction and is firmly packed.

POMANDERS

1 thin-skinned piece of citrus fruit such as an orange,
   lemon, lime or cumquat
thimble or stiletto
60 g (2 oz) good quality whole cloves
1 teaspoon orrisroot powder (available from health food
   stores)
1 teaspoon ground cinnamon
narrow Christmas ribbon

Mark out strips on the fruit that the ribbon will
cover and leave these areas free from cloves.
Carefully press the cloves into the fruit in rows,
making sure they are placed so close together that
they touch. You will need to wear a thimble or
use a stiletto to punch a hole in the fruit before
you push in each clove. Mix the spice powders
together and brush them over the fruit. Wrap the
pomanders firmly in greaseproof paper with the
remaining powder.

Store in a cool, dark place such as a drawer or
cupboard for 4 to 6 weeks to allow the fruit to
dry out and shrink. To speed up this process, a
microwave oven may be used.

To finish the pomanders off, loop the ribbon
around the clear sections of the fruit and tie with
a bow on top. Allow an extra loop for hanging.

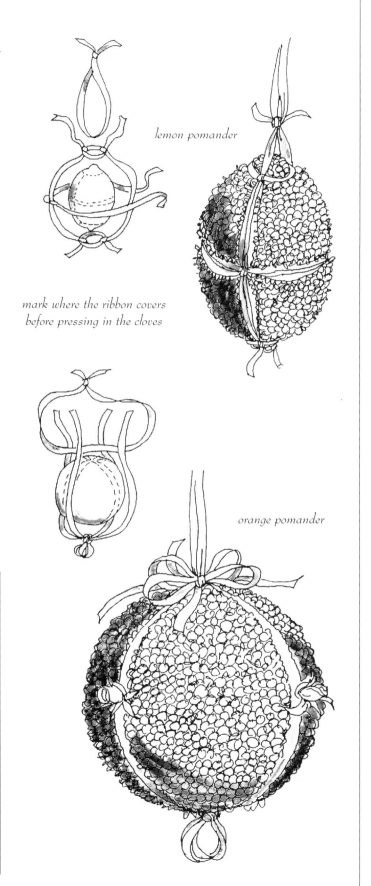

lemon pomander

*mark where the ribbon covers
before pressing in the cloves*

orange pomander

Pomanders

....

*Pomanders made of citrus fruit stuck with
cloves are easy to make and are a fragrant
delight. In England's early days, pomanders
were hung from necklaces or belts to protect the
wearer from foul smells and to supposedly
prevent infection. They look very pretty
trimmed with Christmas ribbon and they add a
lovely spicy scent to the whole room if several
are hung on the Christmas tree. Make small
pomanders from cumquats for hanging on the
tree and for adding interest and perfume to
garlands — or hang them around the house
wherever you want to enjoy their scent.*

PINE CONES

There are so many different decorations you can make from pine cones as they come in such a variety of shapes and sizes and are easy to work with.

🐜 If you want to add a bit of colour to the cones, spray unusually shaped cones with silver or gold paint. These can be used as decorations in a number of ways, and they look wonderful on their own.

🐜 If you have a very large, very open pine cone, file the bottom so it will stand straight and glue dried flowers and other decorations into the gaps to make a miniature Christmas tree.

🐜 Or if you have one that is closed from about the bottom third down, decorate the top with dried flowers so it looks like a small basket full of flowers — use ribbon as the basket handle.

RIGHT: *Festive wreath (page 37) made from a grape vine base and decorated with cumquats and a selection of dried flowers.*
BELOW: *Garland (page 36) made from a grape vine base and decorated with eucalyptus leaves and a variety of Australian nuts and seed pods.*

GIFTS

EDIBLE Gifts

Included in this chapter are recipes
for chutneys, pickles, vinegars,
mustards, jams, jellies,
marmalades, preserved fruits, chocolates,
biscuits and bouquet garni — the sorts
of wonderful gifts that can be enjoyed
all year round. The ingredients used
in these edible gifts are fruits and
vegetables that are in season during
an Australian Christmas.

CHUTNEYS AND PICKLES

PLUM CHUTNEY

2 kg (4½ lb) plums, skinned and stoned
750 g (24 oz) green apples, peeled, cored and chopped
500 g (16 oz) sultanas
1 litre (35 fl oz) cider vinegar
500 g (16 oz) white sugar
2 tablespoons salt
250 g (8 oz) onions, peeled and chopped
1 tablespoon ground cloves
1 tablespoon ground cinnamon
1 tablespoon whole allspice
1 tablespoon ground ginger

Place all ingredients in a heavy non-aluminium saucepan. Stir over a medium heat until the sugar dissolves and simmer for 1 hour, or until it thickens. Pour into hot, sterilised jars, cover and seal. Label, date and store for 4 weeks before use.

GREEN TOMATO PICKLE

1.25 kg (2½ lb) green tomatoes, thinly sliced
2 tablespoons salt
1 litre (35 fl oz) vinegar
½ cup (125 ml/4 fl oz) treacle
1 tablespoon mustard powder
3 teaspoons curry powder
½ teaspoon mixed spice
3 large onions, peeled and thinly sliced
½ teaspoon cayenne

Salt the tomatoes and allow to stand for a day. Place the vinegar, treacle, mustard, curry powder and mixed spice in a large non-aluminium saucepan. Cook gently until almost boiling. Add the tomatoes, onions and cayenne to the saucepan and simmer for five minutes. Pour into hot, sterilised jars, cover and seal. Label, date and store for 4 weeks before using.

PREVIOUS PAGES: *Chutneys and pickles (page 48), vinegars (page 49), mustards, marmalades (page 56) and preserved fruits (page 57).*

PEACH CHUTNEY

½ cup (75 g/2½ oz) chopped onions
500 g (16 oz) raisins, chopped
1 clove garlic, chopped
2 kg (4½ lb) peaches, peeled, stoned and diced
⅔ cup (100 g/3½ oz) fresh ginger, peeled and chopped
2 tablespoons chilli powder
2 tablespoons mustard seeds
1 tablespoon salt
1 litre (35 fl oz) cider vinegar
750 g (24 oz) brown sugar

Place all ingredients in a heavy non-aluminium saucepan. Bring to the boil. Stir and simmer for one hour. Pour into hot, sterilised jars, cover and seal. Label, date and store for 4 weeks before use.

PICKLED ONIONS

small white or pickling onions, similar in size
brine (1 tablespoon of salt to 625 ml (21 fl oz) water)
1 red chilli
Spiced White Vinegar

Soak the onions in brine for 24 hours. Drain and wipe the onions dry. Arrange them in sterilised bottles or jars. Bring sufficient vinegar to the boil to cover the onions. Strain and cool the vinegar and pour it over the bottled onions. Seal, label and date the jars.

To sterilise jars

Wash the jars in hot, soapy water, and rinse thoroughly in boiling water. Put them in a large saucepan and cover with hot water. Cover and bring to a boil, continue boiling for 15 minutes. Leave the jars in the water until just before they are to be used. Invert the jars onto a clean teatowel to dry, then fill. Sterilise the lids for five minutes, or according to the manufacturer's instructions. Fill the jars while they are still hot.

VINEGARS

HERB VINEGAR

Herb vinegar is very easy to make, especially if you grow your own herbs at home. Even if you don't grow your own, herbs are readily available, especially around Christmas time. Mint, thyme, marjoram, basil and tarragon are all suitable, or a combination of several may be used.

Pick young, fresh leaves and wash and dry them if necessary. Place the herbs in wide-necked bottles, using 3 tablespoons of herbs per 1 litre (32 fl oz) of good quality vinegar. Using non-metallic lids or caps, seal the bottles tightly and leave for 3 to 4 weeks. After this time the vinegar should be sufficiently flavoured to strain off into clean, fresh bottles. Don't bottle the herbs used to the flavour the vinegar, but add a fresh sprig of the appropriate herb for decoration.

SPICED WHITE VINEGAR

3 tablespoons black peppercorns
1 tablespoon celery seeds
1 tablespoon mustard seeds
1 tablespoon whole allspice
1 tablespoon mace
1 tablespoon chopped fresh ginger root
2 cloves garlic
¾ cup (185 g/6 oz) white sugar
2 litres (3½ pints) malt, cider or white wine vinegar

This vinegar differs from herb vinegar in that it is heated to aid the extraction of flavour from the spices.

Grind the spices and bruise the ginger and garlic. In a non-aluminium saucepan, very gently heat the spices, ginger and garlic with the sugar and vinegar to just under boiling point. Simmer for 10 minutes. Cool and store in a sealed container in a dark place for 4 weeks. Filter through cheesecloth or a dampened teatowel and bottle for use.

Spiced vinegar is used in a number of pickle and chutney recipes. When making a spiced vinegar, choose a good malt, cider or wine vinegar as the acetic acid content of the vinegar must be at least 5%. White wine vinegar gives a better appearance, but malt vinegar gives a richer flavour to the more spicy chutneys.

RASPBERRY VINEGAR

1½ kg (3 lb) fresh raspberries
1 litre (35 fl oz) white wine vinegar
white sugar (see recipe instructions)

Pick over the raspberries carefully. Place them in a large jar or a china basin. Cover them with the vinegar and allow them to stand in a cool place for 10 days. Stir gently every day.

Strain the flavoured vinegar through a fine nylon sieve or muslin (allow it to drip but do not squeeze the fruit). Measure the vinegar and allow 500 g (16 oz) sugar for every 2 cups (500 ml/ 16 fl oz) of liquid.

Gently bring the vinegar to the boil, add the sugar and simmer for about 10 minutes, skimming any scum that rises to the surface if necessary. Allow the mixture to cool in the pan. Bottle and cork securely. Store in a cool place.

Raspberry vinegar was indispensable in the pantries of the Victorian era, and is once more back in fashion. It may be used to deglaze the juices of roasted poultry, veal or pork dishes and it also gives an interesting dimension to Bearnaise sauce. Serve it in place of tarragon vinegar or, best of all, use it to make a most refreshing summer drink. Place about 1 tablespoon in a glass with ice cubes and top it up with soda water. A jigger of brandy makes it even more delicious!

MUSTARDS

Pots and small jars of mustard make wonderful gifts. They must always be stored in sterilised jars. (See page 48 for instructions on sterilising jars.)

COARSE-GRAINED MUSTARD

1 tablespoon salt
1 teaspoon black peppercorns
1 cup (250 ml/8 fl oz) Vermouth or white wine
1 cup (250 g/8 oz) yellow or black mustard seeds, or a combination of both
1 cup (250 ml/8 fl oz) oil
1 cup (250 ml/8 fl oz) white vinegar
2 teaspoons chopped fresh herbs of your choice

Blend the salt, peppercorns and Vermouth or wine in a food processor until smooth. (These ingredients need to be blended extremely well or separation may occur.) Pour the mixture into a bowl.

Blend together the yellow and black mustard seeds, oil and vinegar. Combine with the first mixture and add the herbs. Pour into sterilised pots or jars (see page 48), cover and allow to stand for several days.

SMOOTH FRENCH MUSTARD

⅓ cup (45 g/1½ oz) English mustard powder
1 tablespoon white sugar
¼ teaspoon salt
2 eggs
⅔ cup (155 ml/5 fl oz) tarragon vinegar

Combine the mustard powder, sugar and salt in a small, ceramic-lined saucepan. Beat the eggs with the vinegar and slowly stir the mixture into the saucepan in a continuous stream. Cook until the mixture is thick and smooth. Allow it to cool in the saucepan and pour it into sterilised pots or jars (see page 48); label and date.

PREVIOUS PAGES: *An assortment of jellies and preserved fruits.*

JAMS, JELLIES AND MARMALADES

A jar of homemade jam, jelly or marmalade is always a welcome gift. The fruit chosen for making jam and jelly should always be barely ripe, preferably under-ripe.

Jam should only consist of fruit, fruit juices and sugar, except in the case of marmalades. No water should be added unless it is needed to make the juices flow or to prevent burning. All added water has to be boiled out, so the more water added the more the jam has to be boiled, otherwise mildew will appear. Always use a wooden spoon, and stir as gently and as little as possible.

Sugar should be hot when added so that it doesn't stop the boiling process. The easiest way to heat the sugar is to heat it slowly in the oven. To prevent spillage and boiling over, never have the pan more than half full.

Most jams are improved by adding a lemon for every 2 kg (4½ lb) fruit. The lemon fruit or the juice may be used. If using whole lemons, wash them first, then halve them and cook with the fruit. Remove before bottling. The lemon juice helps to release pectin which ensures that the syrup will set.

Testing jams, jellies and marmalades for setting

Place a little bit of jam on a cold plate and let it cool. If the jam is ready, the surface will set and wrinkle when pushed in with your fingertip. If you are using a sugar thermometer, be sure to warm it before putting it into hot jam. When the jam's temperature reaches 100°C (210°F), a good set should be assured. Remove the jam immediately from the heat once the gel point has been reached, as overboiling causes darkening and thickens the consistency of the jam.

All jam should be carefully skimmed as soon as scum rises, and a teaspoon of butter added when the sugar has begun to boil will lessen the amount of scum.

Purée or jelly jams should be poured straight into hot sterilised jars. Marmalade and whole fruit jams may be left to cool and settle for about 20 minutes and gently stirred before bottling. Always seal, label and date the jars immediately.

JAMS

FIG JAM

6 kg (13½ lb) figs
4.5 kg (9½ lb) white sugar
2 lemons

Cut the figs up roughly, removing any stalks. Sprinkle with 1 kg (2 lb) sugar and let stand overnight.

Add the juice of the lemons and the whole skins. Boil until tender. Add the rest of the sugar. Boil until the mixture is a golden brown colour. Remove the lemon skins.

Pour the hot jam into warm, sterilised jars (see page 48). Cover while hot. Seal, label and date the jars.

RASPBERRY JAM

2 kg (4½ lb) raspberries
2 kg (4½ lb) white sugar

Place the fruit in a bowl, cover with sugar and allow to stand overnight.

Strain the juice into a non-aluminium preserving pan and boil for five minutes. Add the raspberries and boil the mixture for about 30 minutes, or until setting point is reached.

Pour into warm, dry, sterilised jars (see page 48). Seal, label and date jars.

PLUM JAM

1.5 kg (3½ lb) plums
⅔ cup (155 ml/5 fl oz) water for ripe juicy fruit, or
   1¾ cups (450 ml/14 1/2 fl oz) water for hard fruit
1.5 kg (3 lb) sugar

Wash the plums and remove any stalks. Place the fruit and water (if needed) in a non-aluminium preserving pan and cook slowly until the fruit is tender and slightly mushy. Ripe fruit will take only a few minutes, but harder varieties may take 20 to 30 minutes.

Add the preheated sugar and stir gently until it is completely dissolved. Boil rapidly, removing stones as they surface. Test the jam for setting point after about 10 mintues of fast boiling. Remove from the heat and skim any scum from the top of the jar.

Cool the jam slightly and pour into warm, dry, sterilised jars (see page 48). Seal, label and date the jars.

FRESH APRICOT JAM

2 kg (4½ lb) fresh apricots, stoned (retain half the kernels)
500 g (16 oz) white sugar for every 500 g (16 oz) of fruit
1 large lemon

Blanch the kernels by cracking open the stones and dipping the nuts in boiling water. Remove their skins.

After weighing the fruit, combine equal amounts of fruit and sugar with the washed and halved lemon in a lightly oiled, non-aluminium preserving pan. If the fruit is very dry, add a minimum amount of water to prevent it sticking. Boil until the fruit is tender, about 20 minutes.

Add the heated sugar and stir until it is dissolved. Boil rapidly until setting point is reached. Add the blanched kernels when the jam is almost cooked.

Pour into hot, sterilised jars (see page 48) and seal immediately. Label and date the jars.

JELLIES

When making jelly, wash and dry the fruit but do not remove the cores, peel, stones or stalks; these are all valuable sources of pectin, which helps to set the jelly.

All liquid is eventually strained through a jelly bag. Never squeeze a jelly bag as this will result in dull and cloudy jelly. Use only enough water to prevent burning and to help the juices to flow, and use the back of a wooden spoon to gently mash the fruit.

Always start testing for the setting point within 10 minutes of boiling, after the sugar has been dissolved. (See page 52, 'Testing jams, jellies and marmalades for setting'.)

Skim the jelly and pour it carefully down the sides of hot, sterilised jars. (See page 48 for instructions on sterilising jars.) This helps disperse any air bubbles. Always cover the jars while hot.

PORT WINE JELLY

blood plums, or any dark red plums
water
lemon juice
white sugar (see recipe instructions)
port (see recipe instructions)

Place the plums in a non-aluminium preserving pan with 500 ml (16 fl oz) of water for every 1 kg (2 lb) of fruit. Simmer slowly until the fruit is quite soft, stirring occasionally with a wooden spoon. Strain overnight through a jelly bag.

Measure the liquid and allow the juice of one lemon, 1 kg (2 lb) of heated sugar and ¼ cup (60 ml/2 fl oz) of port for every litre of juice. Place the juice from the plums and the strained lemon juice into a non-aluminium preserving pan and bring slowly to the boil. Add the heated sugar and stir until the sugar is dissolved. Boil rapidly until setting point is reached, testing after 10 minutes (see page 52). Add the port.

Skim the jelly and pour into hot, sterilised jars (see page 48). Seal while hot. Label and date jars.

CRANBERRY, BLACK OR REDCURRANT JELLY

2 kg (4½ lb) berries
1 litre (35 fl oz) water
white sugar (see recipe instructions)

In a non-aluminium preserving pan, place the berries in water and simmer until soft, about 30 minutes, mashing occasionally. Strain overnight through a jelly bag.

Measure the liquid. Place in a preserving pan and bring slowly to the boil. Stir in 500 g (16 oz) sugar for every 2 cups (500 ml/16 fl oz) juice. Stir until the sugar is dissolved. Boil rapidly until the setting point is reached (see page 52).

Skim the surface of the jelly and pour into hot, sterilised jars (see page 48). Seal while hot. Label and date jars.

APPLE OR CRABAPPLE JELLY

2 kg (4½ lb) green cooking apples or crabapples, chopped
2–3 lemons, washed and halved
white sugar (see recipe instructions)
water

Place the apples and lemons in a non-aluminium preserving pan with just enough water to cover. Bring slowly to the boil and simmer for 1 hour, or until the apples are reduced to pulp, mashing occasionally with the back of a wooden spoon. Strain overnight through a jelly bag.

Measure the liquid and place it in a preserving pan. Bring slowly to the boil, stirring in 500 g (1 lb) heated sugar for every 2 cups (500 ml/16 fl oz) juice. Stir well until the sugar is dissolved. Boil rapidly until setting point is reached (see page 52).

Skim the surface of the jelly, and pour into hot, sterilised jars (see page 48). Seal, label and date the jars.

RIGHT: *Crabapple Jelly.*

MARMALADES

Marmalade was originally made from quinces (*marmelada* is the Portuguese word for quince jam, or quinces cooked with sugar). Today, however, marmalade is most popularly made from oranges and orange rind. In 1981 the EEC limited the term 'marmalade' to jams made from citrus fruit, but you can of course make marmalade from any fruit.

Always start testing for the setting point within 10 minutes of boiling, after the sugar has been dissolved. (See page 52, 'Testing jams, jellies and marmalades for setting'.)

Skim the jelly and pour it carefully down the sides of hot, sterilised jars. (See page 48 for instructions on sterilising jars.) This helps disperse any air bubbles. Always cover the jars while hot.

ORANGE MARMALADE

6 oranges
3 lemons
3 kg (6½ lb) white sugar

Finely shred the rind from the oranges and lemons, removing all the pith and pips. Cover the pith and pips with water and simmer for 1 hour; strain and reserve the juice.

Slice the fruit finely, add the shredded peel and cover with water. Add the strained juice from the pith and pips. Soak overnight.

Place the mixture in a preserving pan and bring slowly to the boil. There should be 3.75 litres (6¼ pints) of liquid. Boil until the peel is quite soft and the liquid reduced by half. Heat 3 kg (6½ lb) sugar, add it to the liquid and stir until it is dissolved. Boil rapidly until the syrup thickens when tested (see page 52).

Remove the pan from the heat and skim off any scum from the surface. Pour into hot, sterilised jars (see page 48). Do not stir clear jelly marmalade; just let it stand for a few minutes to allow the fruit to become evenly distributed. Seal, label and date the jars.

CUMQUAT MARMALADE

2 kg (4½ lb) cumquats
1.75 litres (1¾ quarts) water
juice of 1 lemon
2.5 kg (5 lb) white sugar

Slice the cumquats very thinly and reserve the pips. In a small bowl, cover the pips with 1 cup (250 ml/8 fl oz) water and allow to stand overnight. Place the sliced cumquats in another larger bowl with 6 cups (1.5 litres/1½ quarts) water and allow to stand overnight.

Drain the water from the pips (you can leave a few pips in the jam as they turn an attractive bright green) and add it to the soaking cumquats. Place the fruit, water and lemon juice in a non-aluminium preserving pan and bring slowly to the boil. Cook until the fruit is soft, about 45 to 60 minutes. Add the preheated sugar and stir until it is dissolved. Bring back to the boil and continue to boil rapidly until setting point is reached (see page 52).

Remove the pan from the heat and skim the surface of the marmalade if necessary. Allow to stand for 5 minutes. Pour into warm, sterilised jars (see page 48). Seal, label and date jars.

PRESERVED FRUITS

RASPBERRIES IN WHITE RUM

1 kg (2 lb) raspberries
350 g (11½ oz) castor sugar
white rum (see recipe instructions)

Place the raspberries and sugar in alternate layers to fill a sterilised glass jar (see page 48). Pour over enough white rum to cover the fruit. Seal, label and date the jar.

🥄 This is such a simple recipe and one that is perfect for a last-minute gift — or make a few jars and keep them for an unexpected guest.

Preserving fruit in brandy

Any of the following fruits can be preserved in brandy: apricots, cherries, cumquats, damsons, peaches, pears, plums and raspberries.
Use about 375 g (12 oz) white sugar and 1 cup (250 ml/8 fl oz) of water for every 500 g (1 lb) of fruit.
Wash the fruit thoroughly and wipe off any 'fur' (if relevant). Place the sugar and water in a non-aluminium pan and heat until the sugar dissolves. Boil for 10 minutes. Add the fruit and simmer for about 5 minutes. Remove the fruit, draining well, and pack them into two 500 g (16 oz) sterilised jars (see page 48).
Add the brandy to the drained syrup and bring it back to the boil for a few seconds. (For every 2 cups (500 ml/16 fl oz) of cold syrup, allow ½ cup (125 ml/4 fl oz) of brandy.) Gently pour the syrup over the peaches. Seal, label and date the jars. With fruits that have a tough skin, prick them with a darning needle five or six times to allow the brandy syrup to soak through thoroughly.

SPICED ORANGES

4 oranges
½ teaspoon bicarbonate of soda
2 cups (500 g/1 lb) white sugar
1¼ cups (310 ml/10 fl oz) water
½ cup (125 ml/4 fl oz) vinegar
12 cloves
1 teaspoon ground cinnamon

Cut each orange into 3 mm (⅛ in) slices. Place them in a non-aluminium saucepan and cover with water. Add the bicarbonate of soda and simmer for 20 minutes. Drain, discard the fluid and reserve the oranges.

🥄 In a clean non-aluminium saucepan, combine the sugar, water, vinegar, cloves and cinnamon. Stir over a medium heat until the sugar is dissolved. Boil for 5 minutes, add the oranges and simmer for a further 20 minutes. Cool.

🥄 Pack the orange mixture into sterilised jars (see page 48) and seal. Label and date jars. Once Spiced Oranges have been opened, store them in the refrigerator.

MINI PEARS IN SPICED RED WINE

1 litre (35 fl oz) dry red wine
350 g (11½ oz) castor sugar
rind of 1 orange
10 peppercorns
10 allspice berries
10 whole cloves
16–18 very small pears

Place wine, sugar, rind and spices in a non-aluminium saucepan and heat gently until the sugar has dissolved.

🥄 Carefully peel the pears, leaving the stalk intact if possible. Place in liquid immediately. Bring to the boil and simmer for 20 to 30 minutes, occasionally turning the pears.

🥄 Place the pears in warm, sterilised jars (see page 48) and cover with spiced red wine. Cap the jars securely.

HOMEMADE CHOCOLATES

COLLETTES

Cases
125 g (4 oz) dark chocolate, grated
40 foil confectionery cups

Filling
155 g (5 oz) chocolate, grated
¼ cup (60 ml/2 fl oz) cream
50 g (2 oz) unsalted butter
2 egg yolks
rum or brandy, to taste
extra grated chocolate, slivered almonds or chopped nuts
   for decoration

Make the cases: melt the dark chocolate and brush it thickly and evenly inside the foil cups. Chill until set. Remove the chocolate cases carefully from the foil.

Make the filling: place the grated chocolate and cream in a heavy based saucepan. Cook over a low heat, stirring constantly until thick. Remove from the heat. Beat in the butter, a little at a time, add the egg yolks and beat well. Add the rum or brandy. Cool the mixture until it is thick enough to pipe.

Pipe swirls of the mixture into the prepared chocolate cases, sprinkle with the extra grated chocolate, slivered almonds or crushed nuts. Store in the refrigerator in a covered container. Remove from the refrigerator 10 minutes before serving.

Variations: On non-stick paper, roll marzipan out to form a thin rectangle and cut into 6 cm (2½ in) strips. Place the collette filling in a piping bag and, using a 1 cm (¾ in) star-shaped nozzle, pipe a strip of the mixture along the centre of each piece of marzipan. Turn ends in and roll up, brushing the ends with egg white to seal. Using a pastry brush, completely cover the roll with melted chocolate. Slice roll and place pieces in chocolate cases.

TRUFFLES

300 ml (10 fl oz) cream
500 g (1 lb) fresh couverture chocolate or dark cooking
   chocolate, grated

Bring the cream to the boil. Cool until lukewarm. Add grated chocolate and beat with an electric mixer for 5 minutes. Set aside to cool.

To this basic recipe you may add the following variations:

Half to 1 cup (60 g/2 oz to 125 g/4 oz) of desiccated coconut and 1 tablespoon vanilla essence. Shape the mixture into balls. Dip them in melted chocolate and then roll them in cocoa.

Two tablespoons of rum and ½–1 cup (60 g/ 2 oz to 125 g/4 oz) seedless raisins. Shape the mixture into balls and roll them in chocolate threads or sprinkles.

Two to 3 tablespoons of instant coffee stirred and dissolved in hot cream. Pipe the mixture into paper or foil confectionery cups and sprinkle them with chopped nuts.

Three tablespoons of Grand Marnier and ½ cup (60 g/2 oz) ground almonds, or whole blanched almonds ground in a food processor. Shape and roll in finely chopped almonds.

CHOCOLATE-DIPPED ORANGE OR LEMON SLICES

The contrast between the tangy fruit and rich chocolate in this recipe is particularly delicious. Wash and dry a lemon or navel orange. Make deep furrows in the rind down all sides of the fruit and then slice very thinly. Remove pips carefully and leave slices to drain for 1 hour.

Using a small spatula, spread one side of each slice with melted chocolate, covering only the flesh of the fruit and leaving the serrated edges of the rind and pith showing. Allow slices to dry and, when the chocolate has set, turn them over and repeat on the other side.

RIGHT: *Gingerbread Men (page 60).*

BISCUITS

TRADITIONAL DUTCH CHRISTMAS BISCUITS

2½ cups (310 g/10 oz) plain flour
¾ cup (90 g/3 oz) icing sugar
pinch of salt
250 g (8 oz) unsalted butter
2 teaspoons vanilla essence
1 egg, beaten
½ cup (60 g/2 oz) chopped almonds
⅓ cup (90 g/3 oz) coarsely ground
  sugar cubes

In a large bowl, sift together the flour, icing sugar and salt. Rub the butter in with your fingertips. Add the vanilla essence and 1 tablespoon of the beaten egg. Mix to a dough and knead until smooth. Form the dough into a ball. Wrap the dough in a clean teatowel and refrigerate for at least 1 hour.

&. Roll the dough out on a lightly floured board to 3 mm (⅛ in) in thickness. Dip a 5.5-cm (2¼-in) biscuit cutter in flour and cut the dough into circles. Cut out the centre of each piece of dough with a 2.5 cm (1 in) round cutter. (You do not have to use a biscuit cutter, a blunt knife dipped in warm water will do, but a biscuit cutter will make the job much simpler and quicker.) Mix the almonds and sugar together, brush the rings of dough with the remaining egg and cover the top of each biscuit with the almond and sugar mixture.

&. Place the biscuits on ungreased baking trays and bake at 190°C (375°F) for 8 to 10 minutes, or until just golden.

&. Pack the biscuits in attractive jars, boxes or biscuit tins as gifts. They also look lovely threaded with a piece of Christmas string and hung on the tree.

GINGERBREAD MEN

4 oz (125 g) butter
½ cup (4 oz/125 g) white sugar
1 egg
⅓ cup (90 ml/3 fl oz) golden syrup
½ cup (125 ml/4 fl oz) milk
1½ cups (185 g/6 oz) plain flour
1½ teaspoons powdered ginger
1½ teaspoons ground cinnamon
¾ teaspoon mixed spice
½ teaspoon white pepper
1½ teaspoons bicarbonate of soda, dissolved in a little
  hot water
icing for decorating

Beat together the butter and sugar. Add the egg and golden syrup and continue beating. Add the remaining ingredients and mix to form a dough.

&. Roll the dough out on a lightly floured board to 3 mm (⅛ in) in thickness. Cut the dough into gingerbread men shapes.

&. Place the dough shapes onto a greased baking dish and bake at 175°C (350°F) for 10 minutes, or until cooked. When the biscuits have cooled, decorate them with icing.

CHRISTMAS BISCUITS

2½ cups (310 g/10 oz) plain flour
½ teaspoon salt
185 g (6 oz) butter, cut in cubes
1½ cups (375 g/12 oz) castor sugar
2 egg yolks
2 teaspoons vanilla essence

Place all ingredients in a food processor and mix to a stiff dough. Chill for 2 hours.

&. Roll the dough out on a lightly floured board to a 5 mm (¼ in) thickness. Cut into shapes, such as angels, trees, bells or stars, place on a greased baking tray and bake at 180°C (350°F) for about 8 minutes.

FINNISH CHRISTMAS BISCUITS

⅔ cup (180 g/6 oz) butter, softened
¾ cup (185 g/6¼ oz) brown sugar
3 teaspoons ground cinnamon
3 teaspoons ground mixed spice
2 teaspoons ground ginger
1 ½ teaspoons ground cloves
1 ½ teaspoons bicarbonate of soda
2 ½ cups (310 g/10 oz) plain flour
¼ cup (60 ml/2 fl oz) water

Beat the butter and sugar until creamy. Add the spices, bicarbonate of soda and flour and mix well. Add the water and mix to a smooth dough. Wrap in greaseproof paper and chill in the refrigerator for 30 minutes.

Lightly flour a board and roll the dough out to 6 mm (½ in) in thickness. Cut into shapes and place on an ungreased baking tray. Bake at 190°C (375°F) for 8 to 10 minutes, or until lightly browned. While still hot, pierce a hole in the top of each shape with a skewer. Cool on wire cooling racks.

Thread thin Christmas ribbon through the holes in the biscuits so they can be hung on the tree. Or pack them into attractive jars or boxes as gifts.

This recipe is ideal for using with biscuit cutters or a roller cutter, as it holds a crisp, clear shape and does not spread.

BOUQUET GARNI

Traditionally, a bouquet garni was made from a bay leaf and sprigs of thyme and marjoram, all wrapped in parsley and tied together with a piece of cotton.

In addition to these herbs, you may add a sprig of basil and tarragon and a little lemon rind. Place them all in a small muslin or calico bag and secure it with string, leaving one end long enough to tie onto the handle of a saucepan. Other herbs which may be used are savory, sage, chives, chervil, rosemary, whole peppercorns, garlic, orange peel and celery.

The combinations are many and take very little time to make. For fish, try combining parsley, fennel stalks and lemon rind with bay leaves; or, for pork and game, add a few crushed juniper berries.

A homemade bouquet garni makes a lovely gift. To prepare it, cut a circle or a square of muslin or calico and pink the edges (if desired). Place one level tablespoon of dried herbs in the centre and tie securely with thin matching string. You can also attach a small card saying which herbs have been used. Keep the bags airtight until ready for use.

CRAFTY Gifts

Homemade gifts are an absolute pleasure to give and to receive. There is nothing like spending time making a special gift for a loved one. Included in this chapter are ideas for making gifts that both adults and children can make and enjoy, including painted plates, salt-and-pepper shakers, puzzles and paper flowers.

AUSTRALIAN WILDFLOWER PLATE

wooden plate

Matisse paints
china red base
black base
cadmium yellow
mars black
cadmium red medium
antique white
antique green
brilliant alizarine
Feast and Watson satin proof varnish

Brushes
2.5 cm (1 in) wide stiff bristle brush
No. 000 liner
3 mm (⅛ in) deerfoot stippler
No. 4 round
No. 600 sandpaper

the stalks with the grey-green mixture. Dip the stipple brush into the yellow, dab off any excess and paint in the wattle. Dip the edge of the stipple brush in alizarine and use to create a shadow. Clean the brush.

Dip the edge of the stipple brush in white and use it to create a highlight. Mix white, alizarine and black, and paint in the gumnuts. Using the liner brush, highlight in white and shade in black. Mix the alizarine to a watery consistency and paint the flowers.

Using the stiff brush, undercoat the plate in china red. Allow to dry and undercoat in black. Sand heavily and lightly in patches.

Use the floral design here — transfer it onto the plate. Mix antique green and a touch of alizarine and black to a soft grey-green. Using the liner brush, paint in all

Using the alizarine and the liner brush, paint in the gum flowers, repeat with red then white. Paint dots around the circumference and red 'C' in centre. Using white, paint in flannel flowers using 'S'-type strokes. Using the green and the liner brush, paint the veins and tips of the petals. Using green and the stipple brush, paint in centres. Use the same method and colours as for wattle, paint in the highlights and shadows. Using the liner brush with green and a side load of white, add the leaves.

Sign your work! Varnish, using three coats of Feast and Watson satin proof varnish.

PAINTED PLATES

plain-coloured ceramic plate
tack cloth
brush
liquid text glossies, in bright clear colours
precut stencil designs (optional)

Wash and dry the plate. Paint on the design, or position the stencil on the plate and carefully paint in the design. Allow the paint to dry. Bake at 165°C (325°F) for 30 to 45 minutes. Remove when cool.

⚐ Try a simple plate first and, as you become more efficient, you can build up complete sets of matching plates.

CHRISTMAS T-SHIRTS

T-shirt
heat and bond
fabric, for appliqué
Demential fabric paints
bells
beads
glitter
scissors
pressing cloth

Prewash the T-shirt and the fabric to be appliquéd. Iron the T-shirt and place a board or a thick piece of cardboard inside it. Fabric pieces should be ironed with their wrong side to the heat and bond, using a hot dry iron.

⚐ Cut out the shapes you want on your T-shirt from the appliqué fabric, leaving the heat and bond attached. Peel off any excess paper. Position the shapes on the T-shirt and iron.

⚐ Secure appliqué shapes with fabric paint around their edges, putting half the paint on the appliqué and half on the T-shirt. Decorate with more paint, or add bows, bells, glitter and beads. Use a fabric glue to secure. Leave to dry. Iron the T-shirt with a pressing cloth. Wash inside out. If the T-shirt is to be a gift, include a card outlining instructions for washing.

WASH BALLS

200 g (6½ oz) soap
¼ cup (60 ml/ 2 fl oz) rosewater, heated
3–4 drops essential oil of lavender
extra rosewater, to finish

Save scraps of leftover soap until you have 200 g (6½ oz); alternatively, buy unperfumed soap. Grate or chop the soap and place it in a basin. Pour the heated rosewater over the soap. Allow the mixture to set in the basin for 10 to 15 minutes.

⚐ Using a wire whisk, beat in one drop of oil at a time; or pour the mixture into a blender and, with the motor running, slowly add one drop of oil at a time. Allow the mixture to cool before pouring it into a container. Leave it undisturbed for 2 to 3 days. When the soap has begun to dry out and set, roll it into small balls and allow them to dry in the sun. When these balls are almost dry, dampen your hands with the extra rosewater and roll the balls until they are shiny and smooth.

Rosewater may be purchased at the chemist, or you may make your own by combining half a teaspoon of essential oil of rose with 5 tablespoons of water.

PREVIOUS PAGES: *The completed Australian Wildflower Plate.*

HESSIAN MICE

hessian
needle and thread
toy fill
strands of hessian
small black buttons for eyes

Cut out a rectangle of hessian and fold it in half. Sew down two sides, leaving one side open. Turn inside out so the stitching is on the inside.

Using a small amount of toy fill, stuff the two top corners and tie them off with a strand of hessian to make two ears. Fill the top third below the ears to make the face and tie at the neck. To make the nose, run thread in a circle in the middle of the face and pull it tight. Sew on the small black buttons for eyes.

Bunch small strands of hessian thread and tie them in the middle to make whiskers, sew them under the nose.

Fill the lower corners for feet and tie as for the ears. Fill the body. Plait strands of hessian to make the tail, sew it on, just inside the lower opening. Sew up the lower opening. Run thread in a circle at the top of the body for arms (as for the nose). Tie a bow at the neck.

WOODEN FRUIT

wooden fruit, such as apples, pears or watermelon
Ceramacoat paint in colours of your choice, such as red
  or green
foam brush
clear spray varnish

Paint the background of the fruit in the colour of your choice — two coats are required. Allow paint to dry between coats. Highlight the fruit by brushing a lighter colour on one side, and smear it with a cloth to blend colours. Leave to dry.

Finish the fruit with a light coat of clear spray varnish. Dry in a dust-free area.

RIGHT: *Hessian Mice.*
BELOW: *Wooden Fruit.*

RED CREPE PAPER FLOWERS

red crepe paper
florist's wire

Make the stamens: cut a 10-cm (4-in) piece of crepe paper roll, cutting across the roll. Refold the paper into four. Make cuts in the refolded paper 5 to 12 mm (¼ to ½ in) in width, leaving 2.5 cm (1 in) uncut. Firmly twist strips.

Make the petals: cut across a 12.5-cm (5-in) crepe paper roll. Undo and refold into four. Cut every 7.5 cm (3 in), leaving 2.5 cm (1 in) uncut. Shape the top of the petal.

To assemble: Take nine or more stamens, gather together and twist uncut ends to hold and wire firmly. Place petals evenly around stamens in layers, gathering as you go. The number of petals used depends on the size of the flower required. Wire firmly, leaving enough wire for a stem. Cover base and wire stem with a 12 mm (½ in) strip of crepe paper, stretching paper as you twist to cover.

To shape the flower: Gently but firmly work the crepe paper petals with thumbs, pushing into the base of the metal, then pull across the outer edge of the petal in the opposite direction, starting with the innermost petals

CHIPWOOD BOXES

chipboard boxes
Delta paint
gold glitter fabric paint
foam brush
sea sponge
clear spray varnish
PVA glue

These boxes are available from craft shops in a wide range of shapes and sizes. They can be decorated in many ways, with folk art paints and decoupage or stencilling, to name just a few. I have chosen a very simple painted finish which looks wonderfully festive.

Using a foam brush, apply two coats of Delta paint to the inside, outside and lid of the box. Allow paint to dry between coats. Using the sea sponge and gold glitter fabric paint, lightly sponge around the outside edge of the lid and leave to dry.

When completely dry, finish box and lid with a light spray of clear varnish. If you wish to attach a decoration to the lid, glue it on with PVA glue.

If using a stencil, first apply two coats of paint to the inside, outside and lid of the box, allowing paint to dry in between coats. Then position the stencil on the lid of the box and, using a sea sponge, sponge paint on the inside of stencil. Allow paint to dry and finish work with a light spray of clear varnish.

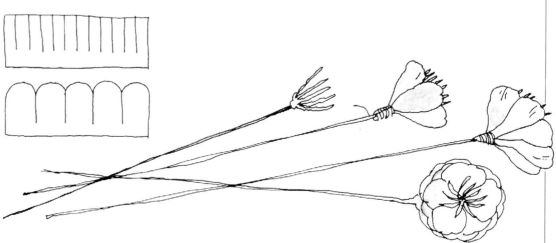

POTPOURRI

Potpourri is an aromatic mixture of dried flowers, leaves, herbs, spices, roots and seeds, originally used to disinfect and deodorise homes. Follow the basic principles and create an infinite variety of mixtures.

Traditional potpourris are made by the 'moist' method. Half-dried petals of flowers are first layered with salt and cured for a few weeks. Then more dried plant material, spices, oils and a fixative are added before further curing takes place. This slow maturing process ensures a long-lasting potpourri, which may last for up to 50 years.

Today, potpourris made by the 'dry' method are more popular. The result is more colourful and usually quicker to produce, if not as long-lasting. For a new effect, try using Australian natives.

Flowers

Flowers give potpourri its aroma, texture and colour. Gather the flowers in the morning after the dew, and before essential oils evaporate. Separate the petals and dry them on paper or netting in a well-ventilated place away from sun. Turn the petals often while they're drying.

Leaves

Scented geranium leaves offer a great range of perfumes. So do lemon verbena, rosemary, lemon balm, thyme, the mints, pineapple sage, eucalypts, bergamot and bay leaves. The thicker leaves should be removed from their stems and dried as petals, but small, thin leaves can be hung in bunches.

Oils

These match or complement the basic perfume of the potpourri. Essential flower oils are concentrated and must be added drop-by-drop, or the whole mixture can be overwhelmed by one perfume. Essential flower oils are available at health food stores.

Spices

Spices add interest and depth to a potpourri, but must be used sparingly. The ones most commonly used are cloves, cinnamon, nutmeg and allspice.

Fixatives

These help retard the evaporation of essential oils and retain fragrance. The main fixative in 'dry' potpourris is powdered orrisroot. It may be obtained from health food stores or pharmacies.

Dried citrus peel, without the pith, is also a useful fixative. Dry in strips or grate. Aromatic wood shavings, such as cedar or sandalwood, may also be used.

Potpourri recipe

8 cups (750 g/1 ½ lb) petals, flowers and leaves, tightly packed
½ cup (60 g/2 oz) powdered spices and powdered fixative
1 cup (120 g/4 oz) dried herbs
6 drops essential flower oil(s) of choice

Simple Dry Potpourri

2 cups (180 g/6 oz) dried rose petals
½ teaspoon ground cinnamon
½ teaspoon crushed cloves
½ teaspoon nutmeg
1 teaspoon dried applemint or Eau de Cologne mint leaves
2 teaspoons orrisroot powder
2–3 drops essential oil of rose

Simply combine the flowers, flower petals and leaves in a large bowl. Add the remaining dry ingredients (herbs and spices), into which the oil has been dropped. Store in a sealed container in a dark, dry place for 6 weeks, stirring occasionally.

Cards, WRAPPING PAPER AND BOXES

O ne of the things that makes Christmas fun is wrapping and unwrapping gifts. There is nothing like spending an evening wrapping and then seeing a pile of beautiful parcels of all shapes and sizes stacked under a Christmas tree. This chapter will guide you as to how to make the most of wrapping and packaging and presenting your gifts using simple and economical ideas.

BOXES AND BOWS

CHRISTMAS CARTONS

milk, juice or cream cartons, empty and thoroughly
    washed
spray adhesive
Christmas wrapping paper
narrow ribbon

Measure and rule a line 13 cm (5 in) up
from the base all around the carton. Mark
the central point on each side and then
mark a point 3.5 cm (1½ in) below and
above these points. Cut out the shape.

🎗 Select an attractive, good-quality
Christmas wrapping paper and cut a strip
slightly longer than the height of the
shaped carton and slightly larger than its
circumference to allow a small overlap.

🎗 Using spray adhesive, glue the
carton and the inside of the paper.
Align the carton on the
paper, allowing a small
overlap at the
base. Slowly
roll the
carton and
firmly
adhere the
paper to the
carton.

🎗 Trim the
paper at the top in
line with the cardboard
and neatly fold the
excess onto the base.
Cut out a square of
paper slightly smaller
than the base. Spray glue the
carton base and the underside of

PREVIOUS PAGES: *The basis for these attractive
packages are bought from craft shops and covered
in the same manner as Christmas Cartons.*

the paper and adhere the paper to the base, neatly
covering the previous
overlapping paper.

🎗 Punch holes in the top
flaps to allow a ribbon to
be threaded through.

🎗 To complete the
gift pack, make a
matching gift card.
Using spray glue, press
matching paper onto
firm cardboard,
fold in centre
and punch a
hole in the
corner to allow a
ribbon to be threaded through.

🎗 Large cartons can be used for gift
boxes. Follow the same instructions as
above, modifying the cutting lines to
fit the size of the carton.

STIFFENED RIBBON OR FABRIC

10 cm (4 in) wide strip of ribbon, or piece of fabric
Petal Porcelain (available at craft shops)

Dampen the ribbon or the fabric with
water and squeeze tightly to remove any
excess moisture.

🎗 Coat the dampened ribbon or
fabric with Petal Porcelain and
again squeeze out the excess. Tie
the ribbon into a bow of any shape
you fancy. Or shape the fabric into
a design of choice — for example,
try making a basket to put your gift
in. If you are giving a bottle of wine
or an edible gift in a jar, shape the
fabric to fit the gift. Place
scrunched-up aluminium foil into
the bow loops or use it to fill the
shape to hold it in position until it
dries. Leave it to dry overnight.

🎗 Remove the foil the following day
when it is completely dry and stiff.

CHRISTMAS BOW

minimum of 1.5 m (4 ft 6 in) of ribbon, cut into two
   lengths of 1 m (3 ft) and 0.5 m (18 in)

Place the parcel in the centre of the 1 m (3 ft)
length of ribbon. Cross the ribbon over with the
right piece of ribbon closest to you. Hold it with
your right hand. With your right hand, tuck the
ribbon over and under and pull it towards you.

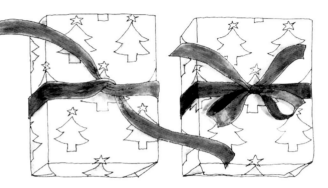

✍ Hold down the centre with your right index
finger. With your left hand, make a 7-cm
(2¾-in) loop with the left ribbon towards your
right finger. Hold the
loop with your
left hand. Bring
the right hand
ribbon over the
loop from the front
to the back to
form the centre of
the bow, with the
wrong side of the
ribbon facing up.
Make a second loop
under the first one,
pulling it through
with your left hand.
Adjust it to face
right-side-up. Simultaneously, pull both loops to
tighten the bow. Adjust and trim off the tails.
✍ Turn the box sideways with the loops to the
right hand side. Take 0.5 m (18 in) of ribbon and
thread it under the bow, with the wrong side of
the ribbon facing up. Repeat stages 1 and 2.

CHRISTMAS CARDS

To make blank cards, ready for decoration, cut
plain cardboard to the required shape and size or
buy packets of plain cards.

You can also use the ideas below to make gift
cards, wrapping paper and decorations.

Stencilling
Trace the outline of any design of your choice
from an old Christmas card, or use a precut plastic
stencil. Colour in the outline with Texta pens,
crayons, coloured pencils or bright acrylic paint.
If you are using paint, place a small amount on a
palette and dab a stencil brush in the paint,
wiping any excess on a scrap of paper. Work paint
well into the brush before carefully dabbing onto
the stencil. Remove the stencil and leave to dry.

Embossed stamping
This method gives a shiny metallic finish. Choose
a rubber stamp design and an embossing powder.
Apply embossing fluid to a dry stamp pad, press
the stamp onto the pad, then press the stamp onto
the paper or card. Sprinkle embossing powder
over the stamped area, dust off any excess powder
and then hold the embossed area of the paper or
card over a heated iron or toaster to set it.

Stamping
There are now many Christmas stamps available,
with coloured, plain, or striped stamp pads. Press
the stamp down onto the surface of the pad
firmly, and apply to the card or paper.

Pressed flowers
Pressed flowers can be used to decorate Christmas
cards but they also make very attractive
bookmarks as gifts.
✍ Cut plain-coloured (or white), lightweight
cardboard to the required size. Place the pressed
flowers or leaves in a design, remove them and
carefully spray the underneath of each flower or
leaf with clear craft glue. Place the flowers or
leaves back into position, this time pressing down
lightly with a clean dry cloth to ensure they
adhere properly.

Quilling

Quilling, or 'paper filigree' is the art of coiling, folding and rolling strips of paper to form pictures and patterns.

HOW TO QUILL

quilling tool (from craft shops)
quill paper (from craft shops) strips
PVA glue
blank cards

Using the quilling tool and paper strips, roll the paper from one end to the other, into a coil. Glue the coil(s) onto the card in the desired design, such as a Christmas tree. Decorate with more quilling paper using gold strips for the pot, for instance — you can really use your imagination with quilling and create whatever picture you want, be it simple or complex.

WRAPPING PAPER

Tie-dyeing

This is a marvellous way to give tissue and crepe paper a completely new 'look'.

🏊 Take a sheet of old or new tissue or crepe paper. Scrunch up small nobs of the paper and twist them into tight peaks. Spray all over paper with paint colour of your choice. The closer the nobs are together, the more patterns will be made. Allow the paint to dry before opening up the paper.

🏊 Alternatively, scrunch up a whole sheet of crepe paper into a tight ball. Spray with paint colour of your choice and allow to dry for a few minutes. Turn the ball over and spray again. Allow to dry before opening out.

RIGHT: *Gift-wrapped parcels, made simply and economically.*
BELOW: *Quilling tool, paper and finished card.*

Stencilling

This technique can be used on brown paper or plain butcher's paper. Try a simple design first – eucalyptus leaves or bracken fern work very well. You can use a few at a time or cover the entire piece of paper with leaves in a pattern.

🐾 Cover your work area with newspaper. Lay the paper down flat, with the right side facing up. Arrange leaves, shells, nuts or ferns on the paper and lightly spray them with gold paint. Allow to dry for a few minutes before moving the plant stencils to another part of the paper. Continue spraying the designs until the whole sheet is covered. Allow to dry for at least half an hour.

FESTIVE FOODS

CHRISTMAS EVE *Buffet*

Christmas Eve is a great time of anticipation and relief that holidays have finally arrived. A buffet dinner is perfect for this occasion and, remember, any leftovers will probably not go to waste as this is the first meal of the festive season. Choose the dishes and wines you prefer from the menu on page 84.

CHRISTMAS EVE BUFFET

CHAMPAGNE PUNCH

GUACAMOLE

CHICKEN LIVER PATE

MARINATED OLIVES

TARAMASALATA

TAPENADE

BORSCHT

GAZPACHO

VICHYSSOISE

AUSTRALIAN DAMPER

COLD SNAPPER
WITH TARRAGON MAYONNAISE

ROAST TURKEY

APRICOT RAISIN STUFFING

MACADAMIA STUFFING

GLAZED HAM WITH CHERRIES

RATATOUILLE EN GELEE

SALAD NICOISE

GREEK SALAD

TABOULEH

CAESAR SALAD

TRADITIONAL CHRISTMAS PUDDING

RICH BRANDY SAUCE

KIPFERLN

AMERICAN CHRISTMAS FRUITCAKE

BAKLAVA

BUCHE DE NOEL

PANETTONE TRADIZIONALE

PANFORTE

SUGGESTED WINES

Sparkling Chardonnay/Pinot Noir:

Yalumba Angus Brut Classic

Dry White:

Richard Hamilton 'Farm Block' Semillon

Dry Red:

Mitchelton 'Print Label' Shiraz

Dessert Wine:

Normans XO Liqueur Tawny 30 Year-old Port

CHAMPAGNE PUNCH

1 cup (250 g/8 oz) white sugar
1¼ cups (310 ml/10 fl oz) water
rind of 1 orange and 1 lemon, grated
juice of 1 orange and 1 lemon
1 cup (250 ml/8 fl oz) grapefruit juice
1 cup (250 ml/8 fl oz) pineapple juice
peel of ½ green cucumber
3 x 750 ml bottles dry ginger ale, chilled
3 x 750 ml bottles lemonade, chilled
1 bottle champagne, chilled
ice cubes
orange, lemon and cucumber slices for garnish

Boil the sugar and water until the sugar has competely dissolved. Add the orange and lemon rind and cool. Add all the fruit juices and cucumber peel. Chill in the refrigerator.

Before serving, add the chilled ginger ale, lemonade, champagne and ice cubes. Garnish with the orange, lemon and cucumber slices.

Makes about 30 glasses.

GUACAMOLE

1 large avocado, peeled, stoned and mashed
1 tomato, peeled and chopped
1 tablespoon finely chopped onion
¼ teaspoon Tabasco sauce
¼ teaspoon dried coriander
¼ teaspoon garlic powder
juice of ½ lemon
salt to taste

Combine all ingredients and mix well. Serve in a bowl, accompanied by Melba toast and raw seasonal vegetables.

Serves 6 to 8.

PREVIOUS PAGES: *Clockwise from the top: Chicken Liver Pâté, Guacamole (with raw vegetables and Melba toast), Marinated Olives (page 88), Taramasalata (page 88) and Tapenade (page 88).*

CHICKEN LIVER PATE

½ cup (125 ml/4 fl oz) beef stock or water
2 teaspoons powdered gelatine
oranges or olives, thinly sliced (optional)
500 g (1 lb) chicken livers
2 tablespoons brandy
60 g (2 oz) butter
4 rashers bacon, finely chopped
2 small onions, finely chopped
¼ teaspoon thyme
1 bay leaf
2 tablespoons dry sherry
4 tablespoons fresh cream
90 g (3 oz) butter, melted

Bring the stock or water to the boil. Add the gelatine and let it dissolve. Cool slightly and pour into a lightly oiled loaf tin. If you want to set the orange or olive slices in the gelatine, pour half the mixture into the tin and refrigerate until set. Arrange the slices on the set gelatine and carefully pour on the remaining liquid. Return to the refrigerator and allow to set. (You can set the mixture in the freezer, it takes about 15 minutes.)

Place the livers in a bowl and pour boiling water over them. Let the water cool. Drain and repeat several times. Remove any tubes from the liver and clean thoroughly to ensure the bitter taste is removed. Soak livers in the brandy.

Melt half the butter in a frying pan and add the bacon, onions, thyme and bay leaf. Cook until tender but not brown. In another frying pan, melt the remaining butter, add the soaked livers and cook, for about 5 minutes, on a low heat. Transfer the livers to the frying pan with the bacon mixture and cook together for 5 minutes. Remove the bay leaf, place the mixture in a food processor and add the sherry. Blend until smooth. With the machine running slowly, add the cream and melted butter. Strain and place the mixture in the oiled loaf tin with the set gelatine. Refrigerate overnight.

Carefully turn out the pâté and serve

Serves 12 to 16.

MARINATED OLIVES

500 g (1 lb) olives
6 tablespoons olive oil
2 tablespoons balsamic vinegar
1 clove garlic, peeled
1 teaspoon chopped oregano

Place all ingredients in a storage jar with a non-metallic lid. Cover and allow to stand for at least 2 days before serving.

Serves 16 to 20.

TARAMASALATA

250 g (8 oz) old potatoes
185 g (6 oz) white bread, thickly sliced
1 cup (250 ml/8 fl oz) warm water
60 g (2 oz) fresh tarama or smoked fish roe
freshly ground black pepper to taste
¾ cup (185 ml/6 fl oz) lemon juice
½ cup (125 ml/4 fl oz) olive oil

Peel, wash and quarter the potatoes. Cover and boil until tender, about 15 minutes. Drain.

Remove the crusts from the bread and place the slices in a large bowl with the water. Let them stand for 5 minutes. Drain the bread and squeeze out as much water as possible.

Place the tarama or smoked roe, potatoes, bread and pepper in a food processor and blend until smooth. Gradually, with the food processor running, add the lemon juice and olive oil. Spoon into serving bowls, cover and refrigerate for several hours. Serve with Melba toast and raw seasonal vegetables.

Serves 8 to 12.

To make garlic croûtons

Remove the crusts from sliced white bread and cube the slices. Fry in butter or oil with a crushed clove of garlic until lightly brown. Drain well on absorbent paper.

TAPENADE

250 g (8 oz) black olives, stoned
100 g (3½ oz) canned anchovy fillets, drained
100 g (3½ oz) canned tuna fish, drained
100 g (3½ oz) canned capers, drained
1 sprig of thyme
1 bay leaf, crumbled
2 large cloves garlic, peeled and halved
2 tablespoons brandy (optional)
4 tablespoons olive oil
freshly ground black pepper to taste

In a food processor, purée all ingredients, except the olive oil and pepper. With the machine running slowly, pour in the oil and add pepper. Serve at room temperature, on slices of French breadsticks (baguettes) or toast.

Serves 8 to 12.

BORSCHT

1 x 450-g (14-oz) can consommé or beef stock
4 raw beetroots, peeled and grated
½ cup (125 ml/4 fl oz) red wine
2 tablespoons tomato paste
2 bay leaves
1 tablespoon lemon juice
salt and cayenne to taste
sour cream, for serving (optional)

Put the consommé or beef stock, beetroots, wine, tomato paste and bay leaves in a saucepan. Bring to the boil and leave to stand for 10 to 15 minutes. Add the lemon juice, salt and cayenne. Serve topped with sour cream.

If you are serving the soup chilled, don't add the lemon juice, salt and cayenne until the last minute — just before serving.

Serves 4.

PREVIOUS PAGES: *Clockwise from the top: Gazpacho, Borscht, Vichyssoise and Australian Damper.*

GAZPACHO

1 cup (250 ml/8 fl oz) chicken stock
3 cups (750 ml/24 fl oz) canned tomato juice
1 large clove garlic, peeled and halved
1 tablespoon tarragon vinegar
3 tablespoons olive oil
salt and freshly gound black pepper to taste
2 green sweet peppers (capsicums), seeded and finely
  chopped
2 cucumbers, peeled, seeded and finely chopped
2 ripe tomatoes, peeled, seeded and finely chopped
2 sticks celery, finely chopped
1 medium white onion, finely chopped
2 teaspoons snipped chives for garnish
garlic croûtons

Combine the chicken stock, tomato juice, garlic, vinegar, oil and salt and pepper in a food processor. Blend until smooth. Cover and chill. Just before serving, stir in the chopped vegetables and sprinkle with the chives. Serve with croûtons.

Serves 6.

VICHYSSOISE

6 large leeks
60 g (2 oz) butter
4 medium potatoes, peeled and sliced
4 cups (1 litre/32 fl oz) chicken stock
salt and pepper to taste
pinch of ground nutmeg
1 cup (250 ml/8 fl oz) fresh cream
whipped fresh cream and snipped chives for garnish

Carefully wash the leeks and chop them into 2-cm (1-in) lengths. Sauté in the butter until soft but not brown. Add the potatoes, chicken stock, salt and pepper and nutmeg. Cover and bring to the boil. Simmer until tender, about 5 minutes.
🥄 Pour the soup mixture into a food processor and blend until smooth. Stir in the cream and chill in the refrigerator.
🥄 Serve with a spoonful of whipped cream and sprinkle with the chives.

Serves 8 to 12.

AUSTRALIAN DAMPER

3 cups (375 g/12 oz) self-raising flour
1 teaspoon salt
1¼ cups (310 ml/10 fl oz) milk
extra milk for glazing

Sift the flour and salt into a large mixing bowl. Form a well in the centre and pour in the milk. Mix with a knife until the dough leaves the sides of the bowl. Knead gently on a lightly floured board. Form the dough into a large ball and place it on a floured baking tray. Cut crosses on the top as desired and brush with a little milk. Place on the bottom of a hot oven (230°C/450°F) and bake for 30 minutes, or until the damper sounds hollow when tapped.

Serves 6 to 8.

COLD SNAPPER WITH TARRAGON MAYONNAISE

1 cup (155 g/5 oz) long-grain rice
grated rind and juice of 1 lemon
2 tablespoons fresh, chopped tarragon
1 large snapper
30 g (1 oz) butter, melted
2 cups (500 ml/16 fl oz) mayonnaise

Cook the rice in boiling water for 10 to 15 minutes. Rinse and drain thoroughly. Add the grated lemon rind to the rice with half the tarragon. Stuff firmly into the snapper.
🥄 Take an oval baking dish, slightly smaller than the fish, and curve the fish, standing upright on the dish. Cover the fins and tail with foil to prevent them from burning. Brush the fish with melted butter and squeeze the lemon juice over it. Bake at 175°C (350°F) for 45 minutes.
🥄 Allow the fish to cool in the dish so it holds its shape. Add the other tablespoon of freshly chopped tarragon to the mayonnaise and serve with the fish. (If you have difficulty in making the fish stand upright when serving, place a layer of cold mashed potato on the serving dish first.)

Serves 8 to 12

ROAST TURKEY

1 turkey
stuffing
3 rashers streaky bacon
butter, melted for basting
salt and pepper to taste

Turkey is a dry bird with very little excess fat, and often the breast meat will cook quicker than the thighs and the legs. There are several ways of preventing this happening but I have found the most reliable way is to lay rashers of streaky bacon over the breast, removing them about 20 minutes before finishing time. The general rule is to allow 15 minutes per 500 g (1 lb) for a bird weighing under 7 kg (14 lb), and 12 minutes per 500 g (1 lb) for a bird over 7 kg (14 lb). (If you're buying a fresh turkey, the meat of a hen is more tender than that of a cock.)

Stuff the neck and body cavities of the turkey. Truss the bird using a packing needle and string, or secure both ends with skewers to prevent the stuffing coming out during cooking. Weigh the bird to estimate the correct cooking time. Baste the turkey with melted butter, season with salt and pepper, and cover the breast with the bacon rashers.

Cook for 20 to 25 minutes at 200°C (400°F), basting frequently. Reduce the heat to 175°C (350°F). Continue to baste. About 20 minutes before finishing time, remove the bacon and allow the breast to brown. Remove the trussing string or skewers and place on a serving dish, keeping the juices to use as a gravy. Garnish with the bacon.

Serves 6 to 8.

> Turkey was first imported to England from South America in the sixteenth century. By the nineteenth century it was being described as "one of the most glorious presents made by the new world to the old".

STUFFINGS

Apricot Raisin Stuffing

3 tablespoons (45 g/1½ oz) butter
1 large onion, sliced
100 g (3½ oz) dried apricots, soaked, drained and chopped
100 g (3½ oz) seedless raisins
grated rind and juice of 1 orange
1 cooking apple, peeled, cored and chopped
2 cups (120 g/4 oz) fresh white breadcrumbs
¼ teaspoon ground ginger
salt and freshly ground black pepper to taste

Heat the butter and gently fry the onion until translucent. Turn the onion into a bowl and stir in the remaining ingredients. Allow to cool before using.

Macadamia Stuffing

2 eggs, lightly beaten
pinch of salt
2 cups (120 g/4 oz) fresh white breadcrumbs
2 cups (185 g/6 oz) boiled rice
2 tomatoes, chopped
2 tablespoons soy sauce
2 medium-sized onions, finely chopped
1 cup (125 g/4 oz) finely chopped macadamia nuts
2 tablespoons chopped fresh herbs or 2 teaspoons mixed dry herbs

Mix all ingredients together and combine thoroughly. (Halve the quantities to stuff a chicken.)

LEFT: Clockwise from the top: Tabouleh (page 93), Caesar Salad (page 93), Roast Turkey, Greek Salad (page 93), Salad Nicoise (page 93) and Glazed Ham with Cherries (page 92).

GLAZED HAM WITH CHERRIES

Sauce

1 x 250-ml (8 fl-oz) jar cranberry sauce

30 ml (1 fl oz) vinegar

2 teaspoons ground ginger

1 teaspoon mustard powder

30 g (1 oz) butter

Ham

½ ham on the bone

cloves

canned black cherries and parsley for garnish

Make the sauce: place all ingredients in a saucepan and stir over a low heat until smooth.

Remove the rind from the ham and score the fat surface in a diamond pattern, stud the surface with cloves and brush the sauce over. Place on a rack in a baking dish. Bake at 175°C (350°F) for 1 hour, basting frequently with the sauce.

Drain the cherries, and put them into the dish with the ham. Cook for another 10 minutes.

Place the cooked ham on a serving dish and garnish with the cherries and parsley. Pour the remaining juices from the baking dish into a saucepan, reheat and serve separately as a sauce.

RATATOUILLE EN GELEE

1 medium eggplant

salt

olive oil for frying

3 large ripe tomatoes

2 Spanish or brown onions, finely chopped

2 medium zucchini

1 large red sweet pepper (capsicum)

4 cups (1 litre/24 fl oz) aspic

bunch of parsley or other fresh herbs of your choice

Prepare the vegetables: thinly slice the eggplant, sprinkle it with salt and leave it for 1 hour. Squeeze out the juices under cold running water (this takes the bitterness out). Dry the eggplant, chop it into bite-sized pieces and fry it in oil. Drain on absorbent paper. Plunge the tomatoes into boiling water then transfer them to cold water (this makes removing the skin easy). Skin the tomatoes, remove the seeds and chop the flesh. Place the sweet pepper into a very hot oven (245°C/475°F) until the skin blisters. Remove the skin and slice the flesh into rings. Fry the onions in a little oil and drain on absorbent paper. Slice the zucchini into rounds and steam lightly. Pat dry. Allow all vegetables to cool.

Assemble the ratatouille: pour a little aspic into a lightly oiled ring mould and allow to set. Add a decorative layer of zucchini and set again with a little more aspic. Layer in the tomatoes, eggplant, sweet pepper, onions and zucchini until full. Fill to the brim with the remaining aspic. Allow to set in the refrigerator for several hours or overnight. Turn out and decorate with the bunch of parsley or other herbs in the centre.

Serves 10 to 12.

French (vinaigrette) dressing

....

Add one part vinegar to three parts oil plus salt and pepper to taste. Remember, dissolve the salt in the vinegar as it doesn't dissolve in oil.

SALAD NICOISE

1 crisp lettuce
4 tomatoes, cut into wedges
1 green sweet pepper (capsicum), seeded and chopped
1 small white or Spanish onion, chopped
1½ cups (375 g/12 oz) chopped celery
100 g (3½ oz) canned tuna, drained
1 small can anchovy fillets, drained
2 eggs, hard-boiled and cut into wedges
8 black olives, pitted and chopped
½ cup (125 ml/4 fl oz) French dressing

Tear the lettuce into a bowl and add the tomatoes, peppers, onion, celery and tuna. Arrange the anchovies, olives and eggs on top of the tuna. Toss with the dressing.

Serves 4.

GREEK SALAD

Dressing
2 tablespoons olive oil
2 tablespoons lemon juice
2 teaspoons chopped marjoram
salt and pepper, to taste

Salad
½ green sweet pepper (capsicum)
½ red sweet pepper (capsicum)
6 tomatoes, cut into wedges
½ cucumber, diced
1 small onion, thinly sliced into rings
200 g (6½ oz) feta cheese, cubed
90 g (3 oz) black olives, pitted
oregano, chopped for garnish

Make the dressing: combine all ingredients in a screw-top jar and shake well.

Cut sweet pepper into small diamond shapes, add them to the prepared tomatoes, cucumber, onion, cheese and olives and mix well.

Toss with the dressing and sprinkle with freshly chopped oregano before serving.

Serves 6 to 8.

TABOULEH

Dressing
½ cup (125 ml/4 fl oz) lemon juice
½ cup (125 ml/4 fl oz) olive oil
½ teaspoon salt
¼ teaspoon mixed spice
freshly ground black pepper to taste

Salad
1 cup (185 g/6 oz) cracked wheat
1 cup (45 g/1½ oz) chopped parsley
1 cup (45 g/1½ oz) chopped mint
2 cups (625 g/1¼ lb) chopped fresh tomatoes
2 cups (90 g/3 oz) chopped spring onions

Make the dressing: put all ingredients together in a screw-top jar, put the lid on securely and shake well.

Wash and drain the cracked wheat, and soak in a bowl with ½ cup (125 ml/4 fl oz) water, for 1 hour. Drain well. Mix with the parsley, mint, tomatoes, spring onions and dressing. Chill slightly before serving.

Serves 8 to 12.

CAESAR SALAD

2 tablespoons olive oil
2 tablespoons lemon juice
1 teaspoon Worcestershire sauce
salt and pepper to taste
1 large cos lettuce
2 eggs, poached or coddled for 1 minute
croûtons (see page 88)
4 tablespoons grated Parmesan cheese

Combine the oil, lemon juice, Worcestershire sauce and salt and pepper and mix well.

Tear the lettuce into pieces, place it in a bowl and pour the dressing over. Toss gently. Break the eggs over the lettuce and toss again.

Add the cheese and the croûtons and toss again just before serving.

Serves 2 to 4.

TRADITIONAL CHRISTMAS PUDDING

250 g (8 oz) chopped beef suet
1 cup (155 g/5 oz) currants
1 cup (125 g/4 oz) chopped almonds
3 cups (475 g/15 oz) seedless raisins
2 cups (125 g/4 oz) fresh breadcrumbs
1 teaspoon ground cinnamon
1 teaspoon grated nutmeg
½ teaspoon ground cloves
⅔ cup (185 g/6 oz) dark brown sugar
1½ cups (250 g/8 oz) mixed peel
4 egg yolks
1 cup (250 ml/8 fl oz) milk, warmed
½ cup (125 ml/4 fl oz) sherry
½ cup (125 ml/4 fl oz) brandy

Mix together the suet, currants, almonds, raisins, breadcrumbs, cinnamon, nutmeg, cloves, sugar and mixed peel. Allow to stand, covered and in a cool place, for 7 to 10 days.

Make the pudding: beat the egg yolks, add the milk, sherry and brandy and mix thoroughly. Place the mixture in a greased pudding basin and cover securely with buttered greaseproof paper, topped with aluminium foil, secured to the basin with string. This recipe will make 1 large pudding, 3 medium-sized puddings, or 10 to 12 miniature ones. Steam the large one for 6 hours, the medium ones for 4 hours and the miniature ones for 2½ to 3 hours. Serve hot, with Rich Brandy Sauce.

Serves 10 to 12.

RICH BRANDY SAUCE

⅔ cup (155 ml/5 fl oz) fresh cream
2 egg yolks
1 tablespoon raw sugar
75 ml (2½ fl oz) good quality brandy

Combine all ingredients in the top of a double saucepan over gently boiling water. Carefully and continuously, stir the mixture until the sauce thickens. Serve hot.

Serves 4 to 6.

KIPFERLN

1 vanilla bean and castor sugar or sifted icing sugar
250 g (8 oz) unsalted butter
½ cup (125 g/4 oz) castor sugar
2½ cups (310 g/10 oz) plain flour
2 cups (225 g/7 oz) freshly ground walnuts or 1 cup
   (125 g/4 oz) freshly ground, unblanched almonds

Make vanilla sugar or icing sugar by placing the bean in a jar of sugar, tightly seal the jar and leave it at least overnight. (The flavour improves the longer you leave the bean in.)

Cream the butter and sugar and gradually blend in the flour. Stir in the nuts. Roll the dough into a long roll and chill for about 15 minutes.

Cut off small pieces of the dough and shape them into crescents. Place the biscuits on a lightly greased baking tray and bake at 170°C (340°F) for 15 to 20 minutes, or until slightly coloured but not brown. While still hot, roll the biscuits in vanilla sugar. Slide the biscuits onto a wire cooling rack. When they have cooled, roll them in the vanilla sugar again.

Makes 10 to 12.

AMERICAN CHRISTMAS FRUITCAKE

3 eggs
½ cup (125 g/4 oz) castor sugar
¾ cup (90 g/3 oz) self-raising flour
250 g (8 oz) brazil nuts, whole
250 g (8 oz) walnuts, chopped
250 g (8 oz) seedless raisins
250 g (8 oz) glacé cherries
250 g (8 oz) glacé fruits, coarsely chopped

Cream the eggs and sugar. Fold in the flour and add the nuts and fruit, combine thoroughly. Place in a well-greased 20-cm (8-in) tin and bake at 150°C (325°F) for 1½ to 2 hours.

RIGHT: *Clockwise from the top: Kipferln, Baklava (page 96), Panforte (page 97), Buche de Noel (page 96), American Christmas Fruitcake, Panettone Tradizionale (page 97) and Traditional Christmas Pudding.*

BAKLAVA

Syrup

1 cup (250 g/8 oz) white sugar

½ cup (125 ml/4 fl oz) water

1 tablespoon lemon juice

2 tablespoons honey

5 cm (2 in) cinnamon stick

3 cloves

Baklava

250 g (8 oz) unsalted butter, melted

500 g (1 lb) filo pastry

2 cups (250 g/8 oz) pistachio nuts or walnuts, finely chopped

1 cup (125 g/4 oz) almonds, finely chopped

2 tablespoons white sugar

Make the syrup: place all syrup ingredients in a saucepan and stir over a low heat until the sugar has completely dissolved. Bring the mixture to the boil and gently simmer until you have a thick syrup, for about 5 minutes. Strain and set aside to cool.

Make the baklava: grease a 33 x 23 x 5-cm (13 x 9 x 2-in) baking dish with the unsalted, melted butter. Line the baking dish with half the filo pastry, one layer at a time. Brush each layer with the melted butter. Mix the nuts and sugar together and spread them evenly over the pastry. Cover with the remaining pastry sheets, again brushing each layer with melted butter. Using a sharp knife, cut through the top layer of filo diagonally to make diamond shapes (make sure you do not cut all the way through to the bottom layer of pastry).

Bake at 175°C (350°F) for 30 minutes. Increase the heat to 220°C (425°F) and bake for a further 15 minutes, or until the pastry is puffed and brown. Remove the baking dish from the oven and spoon the cool syrup over the pastry.

Allow the pastries to cool — now complete cutting through the diamond shapes in the pastry, through all layers, to form individual pieces. Serve when cool.

Serves 6 to 12.

BUCHE DE NOEL

Cake

4 eggs, separated

4 tablespoons castor sugar

¼ cup (30 g/1 oz) cornflour

¼ cup (30 g/1 oz) cocoa

chocolate icing

Filling

250 ml (8 fl oz) fresh cream, whipped

1 tablespoon brandy or rum (optional)

Beat the egg yolks and sugar until thick and creamy. Gradually blend in the cornflour and cocoa. In a separate bowl, whisk the egg whites until stiff and fold them quickly into the mixture. Pour the mixture into a well-greased and lined 28 x 20 cm (11 x 8 in) Swiss roll tin. Make sure the mixture is spread evenly into the corners.

Bake at 190°C (375°F) for 15 to 20 minutes, or until it is dry in the centre. Turn the cake out onto a board covered with a damp, clean tea-towel. Roll up the cake in the teatowel and leave it to cool. Do not roll the cake too tightly. Unroll and carefully remove the teatowel. Spread the cake with stiffly whipped cream (with the brandy or rum folded in, if you like). Roll it up again and cover it completely with chocolate icing. Using a fork dipped in boiling water, make lines along the cake to resemble rough bark.

Make two or three of these logs and lay them on a flat plate to resemble the branches of a tree. Decorate the logs with ivy leaves or small Christmas decorations. This cake, filled and iced, will freeze perfectly.

Serves 6 to 12.

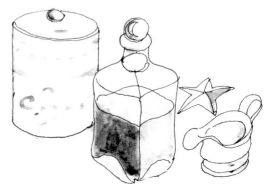

PANETTONE TRADIZIONALE

1 cup (155 g/5 oz) candied fruit
1 cup (155 g/5 oz) seedless raisins
2 tablespoons dark rum
90 g (3 oz) compressed yeast
¼ cup (60 ml/2 fl oz) lukewarm water
1 teaspoon castor sugar
2 whole eggs
3 egg yolks
⅓ cup castor sugar
6 cups (750 g/24 oz) plain flour
1 teaspoon salt
rind of 1 small lemon and 1 small orange, grated
90 g (3 oz) butter, softened
1 tablespoon oil
250 ml (8 fl oz) lukewarm milk
beaten egg for glaze
coarsely ground sugar cubes for sprinkling

Soak the fruit in the rum for about 1 hour. Combine the yeast, water and castor sugar. Stand the mixture in a warm place for about 5 minutes or until it begins to froth. Beat together the eggs, egg yolks and sugar. Sift the flour and salt into a large bowl, add the lemon and orange rind, butter and oil. Stir in the egg mixture, yeast mixture and, finally, the fruit and rum. Beat with a wooden spoon for 5 minutes, or until the mixture leaves the sides of the bowl. Cover with plastic wrap and let stand in a warm place for about 40 minutes, until the dough has doubled in size.

🍯 Place the dough on a floured board and knead for 7 to 10 minutes or until the dough is no longer sticky. Place the dough in a well-greased, high-sided, 6 litre (72 fl oz) ovenproof dish, cover and stand in a warm place for 50 minutes, or until dough has doubled in size.

🍯 Brush the top of the dough with lightly beaten egg and bake at 190°C (375°F) for 15 minutes. Reduce the heat to 180°C (355°F) and bake for a further 1 hour.

🍯 Remove the panettone from the dish and place it on a wire cooling rack. When it has cooled, sprinkle the top with the ground sugar.

Serves 6 to 12.

PANFORTE

rice paper
60 g (2 oz) shelled hazelnuts
100 g (3½ oz) almonds, blanched
75 g (2½ oz) walnuts
45 g (1½ oz) plain flour
1 teaspoon ground cinnamon
pinch each of nutmeg, coriander and ground cloves
45 g (1½ oz) dried apricots, chopped
100 g (3½ oz) mixed peel
½ cup (125 g/4 oz) castor sugar
1 tablespoon honey
icing sugar and cinnamon, sifted for dusting

Line an 18-cm (7-in) cake tin with rice paper, just a little larger than the base. Roast the hazelnuts at 180°C (350°F) for 10 minutes, rub off the skins, then chop the nuts. Roast the almonds until golden brown. Coarsely chop the walnuts. In a mixing bowl, combine all the nuts, the flour, spices, apricots and mixed peel.

🍯 Place the sugar and honey in a pan and stir over a low heat until the sugar is dissolved. Boil for 3 to 4 minutes and then pour it into the nut mixture and stir well. Spoon the mixture into the prepared cake tin and press the ingredients down firmly. Bake at 170°C (325°F) for 35 minutes on the middle shelf. Cool the cake for about 15 minutes, then run a knife dipped in boiling water around the edges to loosen it from the pan.

🍯 When cool, dust with the icing sugar and cinnamon. (This can be made a couple of weeks before Christmas and stored in a cool place.)

Serves 8.

Christmas
BREAKFAST

Christmas morning is full of joy and excitement. It is the ideal time to sit down to a lovingly prepared breakfast and talk about plans for the rest of the day. Choose the dishes you want to include from the menu on page 100. It is up to you whether you cook a full breakfast or just have a simple one of fruit, eggs and toast.

CHRISTMAS BREAKFAST

BUCK'S FIZZ

MELON FRUIT BASKET

EGGS BENEDICT

SCRAMBLED EGGS AND SMOKED SALMON

WAFFLES

MANDARIN MACADAMIA WAFFLES

GINGERBREAD WAFFLES

FRENCH TOAST

MOIST BANANA BREAD

ORANGE BREAD

SULTANA, NUT AND HONEY BREAD

BERRY MUFFINS

DATE AND PECAN MUFFINS

CARROT AND ORANGE MUFFINS

MUESLI AND APPLE MUFFINS

COFFEE AND CREAM

SUGGESTED WINE

Sparkling Burgundy:

Temple Bruer Vintage

BUCK'S FIZZ

100 ml (3½ fl oz) fresh orange juice
1 teaspoon grenadine
¾ cup (200 ml/6½ fl oz) sparkling white wine or
  champagne, chilled
1 lime, thinly sliced

Place the orange juice and grenadine in chilled glasses and top up with wine. Add the slices of lime to decorate and serve immediately, while still chilled.

Serves 2.

MELON FRUIT BASKET

1 cantaloupe or honeydew melon
raspberries, picked over
lychees, peeled and stoned
strawberries, hulled

Draw a faint line around the melon, about two-thirds of the way up from the base. Draw two parallel lines, from side to side, about 2 cm (1 inch) apart, all the way over the top of the melon and down to reach the line on the other side. These lines form the outline of the handle. Cut a small slice from the base of the melon to give it a flat, even surface so it will stand upright without wobbling or falling over.

⚶ With a sharp knife, cut along the two lines that go over the top of the melon to form the handle. With the point of the knife, make a diagonal cut through both sides of the melon, just below the line that has been drawn around the melon. Remove the two wedge shapes of melon and reserve for the filling. Carefully cut the melon flesh away from underneath the carved handle, leaving a smooth under-surface.

⚶ Scrape away the seeds. With a melon-baller, scoop out rounds as close to each other as possible. Mix melon balls with prepared fruits and spoon into the melon basket. (Any seasonal fruits may be used, in any combination you like.)

Serve one melon per person.

EGGS BENEDICT

Sauce
1 cup (250 ml/8 fl oz) sour cream
salt and pepper to taste
2 cups grated cheddar cheese

Base
about 500 g (1 lb) cooked ham or bacon, thinly sliced
6 English muffins, halved
12 eggs, poached

Make the sauce: in a saucepan, slowly warm the sour cream and salt and pepper. Gradually add the cheese, stirring constantly until blended and heated through.

⚶ Lightly fry the ham or bacon and keep hot. Lightly toast the muffin halves. Cover each muffin-half with ham or bacon, drain the eggs and place them on the muffin. Cover with the sauce and serve immediately.

Serves 6 to 12.

SCRAMBLED EGGS AND SMOKED SALMON

4 eggs
8 tablespoons milk (2 tablespoons per egg)
salt and pepper to taste
hot toast for serving
4 large, thin slices smoked salmon
chives, snipped

Beat the eggs, milk and salt and pepper together. Pour them into a hot buttered pan, reduce the heat and cook slowly until firm, stirring frequently with a wooden spoon. Serve the eggs on warm individual plates with a slice of smoked salmon and toast. Sprinkle the eggs with chives.

Serves 4.

PREVIOUS PAGE: *Breakfast table, set with Buck's Fizz, Melon Fruit Basket, Eggs Benedict, Scrambled Eggs and Smoked Salmon, French Toast (page 104) and Cumquat Marmalade (page 56).*

WAFFLES

3 cups (375 g/12 oz) self-raising flour
2 tablespoons white sugar
pinch of salt
3 eggs
2½ cups (625 ml/20 fl oz) milk
60 g (2 oz) butter, melted
maple syrup and/or butter for serving

Sift the flour, sugar and salt into a large mixing bowl. Beat the eggs and milk and add to the dry ingredients. Beat briskly until smooth and add the melted butter. Leave to stand for 1 to 2 hours before using. Cook in a waffle iron as directed and serve with maple syrup and/or butter.

Makes 10 to 12 waffles.

RIGHT: *Scrambled Eggs and Smoked Salmon (page 101).*
BELOW: *Melon Fruit Basket (page 101).*

MANDARIN MACADAMIA WAFFLES

1½ cups (185 g/6 oz) plain flour
2 tablespoons baking powder
pinch of salt
2 tablespoons white sugar
3 eggs
¾ cup (185 ml/6 fl oz) mandarin juice
½ cup chopped macadamias
rind of 2 mandarins, grated
maple syrup and/or butter for serving

Sift the flour and baking powder into a mixing bowl. Mix in the salt and sugar. Form a well in the centre and add the wet ingredients. Stir until the mixture is blended. Stir in the nuts and mandarin rind. Cook in a waffle iron as directed and serve with maple syrup and/or butter.

Makes 10 to 12 waffles.

GINGERBREAD WAFFLES

2 eggs, separated
2 cups (500 ml/16 fl oz) buttermilk
1 cup (125 g/4 oz) wholemeal plain flour
¾ cup (90 g/3 oz) cornmeal
2 teaspoons baking powder
1 teaspoon bicarbonate of soda
½ teaspoon salt
2 tablespoons white sugar
¼ cup (30 g/1 oz) wheatgerm
3 tablespoons finely chopped fresh ginger or 1 teaspoon powdered ginger
6 tablespoons (90 g/3 oz) melted butter or margarine
maple syrup and/or butter for serving

Beat the egg yolks and buttermilk together. Sift the dry ingredients into a mixing bowl, add the ginger and make a hollow in the centre. Gradually add the egg mixture and beat until smooth. Stir in the melted butter or margarine. Whisk the egg whites until they form soft peaks and fold them into the batter. Cook in a waffle iron as directed and serve with maple syrup and/or butter.

Makes 10 to 12 waffles.

FRENCH TOAST

4 eggs
1 cup (250 ml/8 fl oz) milk
2 tablespoons white sugar
1 teaspoon vanilla essence
¼ teaspoon ground nutmeg
8 slices thick bread of your choice
wedges of orange for serving

Beat together the eggs, milk, sugar, vanilla and nutmeg. Dip the bread slices into the mixture and place them on a lightly buttered baking tray. Let them stand for a few minutes.

🥄 Bake at 245°C (475°F) until nicely browned on one side, then turn over. Bake for a further 5 minutes, or until brown. Serve hot with wedges of orange for squeezing over the toast.

MOIST BANANA BREAD

1½ cups (185 g/6 oz) plain flour
1 teaspoon salt
1 teaspoon bicarbonate of soda
3 bananas, peeled and mashed
1 cup (200 g/7 oz) castor sugar
1 egg
¼ cup (60 g/2 oz) butter or margarine, melted

Sift the flour, salt and bicarbonate of soda into a mixing bowl and set aside.

🥄 In a second bowl, combine the bananas and sugar. Add the egg and melted butter or margarine and mix well. Add the banana mixture to the dry ingredients and stir until just moistened.

🥄 Pour the batter into a lined and greased loaf tin and bake at 175°C (350°F) for about 55 to 60 minutes, or until cooked. Cool the bread in the tin for about 10 minutes before turning it out.

Freezing French toast

If you want to prepare French toast before the morning of the breakfast, freeze the slices of bread after they have been dipped into the egg mixture and drained. To cook the frozen slices, place them on a greased baking tray, brush them with melted butter and bake as per the recipe on this page.

ORANGE BREAD

1 cup julienned (chopped into matchstick strips)
   orange rind
1¾ cups (400 g/13 oz) white sugar
4 cups (500 g/1 lb) plain flour
4 teaspoons baking powder
pinch of salt
90 g (3 oz) unsalted butter
1 egg
2 cups (500 ml/16 fl oz) milk

Place the orange rind in a pan and cover it with cold water, bring to the boil and simmer until the rind is soft. Add 1 cup (250 g/8 oz) of sugar and cook the mixture slowly until it forms a syrup — usually for about 10 minutes on a medium to low heat. Drain off the liquid and set the rind aside to cool.

Sift the flour, baking powder and salt into a large mixing bowl. Cream the butter and the remaining sugar and beat in the egg. Add the milk and the sifted dry ingredients and beat for about 4 to 5 minutes. Add the orange rind and continue beating by hand until the mixture is smooth and shiny, about 3 to 4 minutes. Pour the mixture into 2 x 500-g (1-lb) loaf tins, lined and greased, and bake at 175°C (350°F) for 55 to 60 minutes, or until cooked.

SULTANA, NUT AND HONEY BREAD

125 g (4 oz) butter or margarine, softened
½ cup (90 g/3 oz) firmly packed brown sugar
2 eggs
½ cup (125 ml/4 fl oz) honey
½ cup (125 ml/4 fl oz) buttermilk
2 cups (250 g/8 oz) plain flour
1 teaspoon bicarbonate of soda
½ teaspoon powdered ginger
½ teaspoon ground cloves
2 teaspoons cinnamon
¼ teaspoon salt
½ cup (90 g/3 oz) sultanas
½ cup (60 g/2 oz) chopped walnuts

Beat together the butter and sugar until light and smooth. Add the eggs, one at a time, and beat until fluffy. Mix in the honey and buttermilk.

Sift the dry ingredients and stir them into the butter mixture. Fold in the sultanas and nuts and pour the mixture into a lined and greased loaf tin. Bake at 175°C (350°F) for 1 hour, or until cooked. Let the bread cool in the tin for about 10 minutes before turning out onto a wire cooling rack.

BERRY MUFFINS

3 cups (375 g/12 oz) plain flour
½ cup (125 g/4 oz) castor sugar
1 tablespoon baking powder
½ cup (90 g/3 oz) brown sugar
125 g (4 oz) butter or margarine, melted
3 eggs, lightly beaten
1 cup (250 ml/8 fl oz) milk
1½ cups (185 g/6 oz) blueberries, raspberries or any
   berry of your choice

Sift the dry ingredients into a mixing bowl, stir in the brown sugar and make a well in the centre. Add the melted butter, eggs and milk and gently stir in. Lightly fold in the fruit until just combined. Spoon into 12 greased muffin pans and bake at 200°C (400°F) for 20 minutes, or until browned.

Makes 12.

DATE AND PECAN MUFFINS

1 cup (250 g/8 oz) plain wholemeal flour
½ cup (125 g/4 oz) self-raising flour
pinch of salt
2 teaspoons baking powder
1 cup (155 g/5 oz) oat bran
½ cup (125 ml/4 fl oz) buttermilk or milk
2 tablespoons brown sugar
60 g (2 oz) butter, melted
1 egg, beaten
½ teaspoon vanilla essence
½ cup (60 g/2 oz) chopped dates
½ cup (60 g/2 oz) chopped pecans

Sift the flours, salt, baking powder and bran into a mixing bowl. Make a well in the centre. Combine the buttermilk, sugar and melted butter. Stir gently and add the egg and vanilla. Add the dates and pecans to the wet mixture and stir lightly into the dry mixture. Spoon into 12 greased muffin pans until three-quarters full and bake at 200°C (400°F) for 20 to 25 minutes.

Makes 12.

CARROT AND ORANGE MUFFINS

2 cups (250 g/8 oz) self-raising flour
½ cup (125 g/4 oz) wholemeal self-raising flour
½ cup (125 g/4 oz) castor sugar
1½ cups (125 g/4 oz) grated carrot
2 eggs, lightly beaten
90 g (3 oz) butter, melted
½ cup (125 ml/4 fl oz) milk
1 teaspoon grated orange rind
½ cup (125 ml/4 fl oz) fresh orange juice

Sift the flours and sugar into a mixing bowl. Combine the remaining ingredients and add to the flour and sugar mixture. Stir lightly until just combined. Spoon into 12 greased muffin pans and bake at 190°C (375°F) for about 25 minutes.

Makes 12.

MUESLI AND APPLE MUFFINS

1 cup (125 g/4 oz) self-raising flour
1 cup (125 g/4 oz) wholemeal self-raising flour
1 teaspoon ground cinnamon
1 teaspoon ground ginger
¼ teaspoon bicarbonate of soda
1 cup (155 g/5 oz) muesli
¼ cup (90 g/3 oz) sultanas
¼ cup (30 g/1 oz) chopped dried apricots
1 apple, peeled and grated
1 egg, lightly beaten
3–4 tablespoons canola oil
3–4 tablespoons maple syrup
½ cup (125 ml/4 fl oz) apple juice
extra muesli mixed with ¼ cup (125 g/4 oz) raw sugar

Sift the flours, spices and bicarbonate of soda into a large mixing bowl and add the muesli, dried fruits and grated apple. Add the egg, oil, maple syrup and apple juice and stir until lightly blended. Spoon into 12 greased muffin pans. Top each muffin with the muesli and raw sugar mixture and bake at 200°C to 220°C (400°F to 425°F) for about 25 minutes.

Makes 12.

MELALEUCA MORNING

JEFF GUESS

Come and see the light break come watch the sun
Here on this new day Christmas begun
Start from the dark branch crown of a king
Flowers of purple blossom and cling.
Melaleuca morning mantle
Cascades from the heat and night
Bears upon its royal holly
Birth of peace and love and light.
Out of the old wood twisted and hard
Song of December silent unheard
Bursts like a promise onto the stem
Amidst the sharp leaves new life begun.
Melaleuca morning sunrise
From the years of drought and storm
From the hours of heat and darkness
The Lord of love and life is born.
Sun splash in forest from land and scrub
Parkland and city backstreets and drab
Late in the season flame from the earth
Trees that are bearing signs of his birth.
Melaleuca morning matins
Magpies carol from the lawn
All created earth is singing
The child of hope and light is born.

CHRISTMAS DAY
Picnic

T here is nothing like spending Christmas Day relaxing over a leisurely picnic in the Australian bush. Be sure to find a cool, shady spot where everyone will be comfortable. By preparing well before the event you can make this a really festive occasion. Select your dishes and wine from the menu on page 108 and enjoy a Christmas Day picnic outdoors.

CHRISTMAS DAY PICNIC

PEACH PUNCH

FENNEL MARINATED GREEN OLIVES

BRAN DAMPER

CHEESE LOAF

FRESH VEGETABLE TERRINE

CHICKEN AND ORANGE LOAF

CHICKEN FILLETS WITH MANGO MAYONNAISE

COLD CRUMBED CUTLETS

POTATO TORTILLA

HOMEMADE MAYONNAISE

WATERCRESS MAYONNAISE

MESCULIN SALAD

ORANGES IN COINTREAU

LIGHT CHRISTMAS CAKE

BAKEWELL TARTS

MOIST GINGERBREAD CAKE

SUGGESTED WINES

Dry White:

Draytons Hunter Valley Verdelho

Soft Dry Red:

Shottesbrook McLaren Vale Merlot

PEACH PUNCH

6 ripe peaches
1 cup (250 g/8 oz) white sugar
4 bottles Riesling
ice cubes
extra peaches, sliced for decoration

Peel the peaches, slice them into a small bowl and sprinkle them with sugar. Pour over the Riesling, cover and chill overnight.

Just before serving add the ice. Decorate with the extra peaches. (Other fruits such as apricots, nectarines or strawberries can also be used.)

Makes about 24 glasses.

FENNEL MARINATED GREEN OLIVES

250 g (8 oz) green olives
3 bay leaves
1–2 sprigs fennel
1 teaspoon fennel seeds
piece of dried orange rind
olive oil to cover

Place the olives, herbs and rind in a suitable storage jar and cover with the olive oil.

Allow to stand for at least 1 week before serving.

Serves 8 to 10.

Be prepared

Try to keep everything very simple and prepare ahead of time as much as possible so you are not trying to butter the bread rolls before the butter has melted and the ants have started on the food before you!
Have the salads ready in their bowls and the meats carved and covered on their platters. The extra time spent at home organising the picnic will save a great deal of frustration when you finally arrive at your destination.

BRAN DAMPER

¼ cup (30 g/1 oz) self-raising flour
1 teaspoon salt
¼ cup (30 g/1 oz) powdered milk
¾ cup (90 g/3 oz) bran
1¾ cups (420 ml/14 fl oz) water

Combine the dry ingredients, form a well in the centre and pour in the water. Mix with a knife until the dough leaves the sides of the bowl. Knead gently on a lightly floured board. Form into a large ball and brush with a little milk. Place in the bottom of a very hot oven at 230°C (450°F) and bake for 30 minutes, or until the damper sounds hollow when tapped. For the best results, serve the same day the damper is baked

CHEESE LOAF

2 cups (250 g/8 oz) self-raising wholemeal flour
2 teaspoons celery salt
pinch of pepper
15 g (½ oz) butter or margarine
1 egg, lightly beaten
⅔ cup (155 ml/5 fl oz) milk
1 cup (125 g/4 oz) grated cheese

Sift the flour, celery salt and pepper into a large mixing bowl. Rub in the butter or margarine with your fingertips. Stir in the egg and milk. Add three-quarters of the cheese and mix well. Turn into a lined and greased loaf tin and sprinkle the remaining cheese on top. Bake at 200°C (400°F) for 35 minutes. Wrap in foil and keep warm for your picnic.

PREVIOUS PAGES: A cool, shady spot by the water is an ideal place for a bush picnic. Pictured here are, clockwise from the top left: in the basket, the Moist Gingerbread Cake, Bakewell Tarts and Light Christmas Cake (page 120); Oranges in Cointreau (page 117); Peach Punch; Fennel Marinated Green Olives; Potato Tortilla (page 117); Cold Crumbed Cutlets and Chicken Fillets with Mango Mayonnaise (page 116); Fresh Vegetable Terrine (page 114); and, in the centre of the setting, Mesculin Salad (page 117).

FRESH VEGETABLE TERRINE

250 g (8 oz) carrots, peeled and thinly sliced

250 g (8 oz) white radishes or zucchini, peeled and thinly sliced

250 g (8 oz) broccoli, broken into small florets, or green beans, thinly sliced

2 tablespoons powdered gelatine

2 cups (500 ml/16 fl oz) homemade chicken stock (or use 2 chicken stock cubes to make 2 cups stock)

Plunge the vegetables into rapidly boiling water and simmer for 5 minutes. When they are just cooked, plunge them immediately into ice water and drain. Dissolve the gelatine in the stock and strain it into a large jug to make aspic.

Lightly oil a loaf tin or terrine. Pour in a thin layer of aspic and allow it to set in the refrigerator. Place the individual vegetables into the jug of aspic and coat them with the aspic, remove them with a slotted spoon and lay them neatly on the already-set aspic. Repeat with each type of vegetable until the tin is almost full with layered vegetables. Pour over the remaining aspic and refrigerate until set.

Turn out when set and serve in thick slices with Watercress Mayonnaise (page 117).

Serves 8.

ABOVE: *Fresh Vegetable Terrine and Watercress Mayonnaise (page 117).*
RIGHT: *Potato Tortilla (page 117) and Mesculin Salad (page 117).*

CHICKEN AND ORANGE LOAF

375 g (12 oz) chicken breast fillets

90 g (3 oz) chicken livers

2 rashers bacon, rind and bones removed

1 clove garlic, crushed

2 spring onions, finely chopped

1 egg yolk

¼ cup (30 g/1 oz) dry breadcrumbs

rind and juice of 1 orange

2 tablespoons chopped parsley

1 sheet ready-rolled puff pastry

1 egg, beaten for glazing

Trim the chicken and cut it into 5-cm (2-in) pieces. Trim the chicken livers. Cut the bacon into quarters. Mince the chicken, chicken livers and bacon together in a food processor. Combine with garlic, spring onions, egg yolk, breadcrumbs, orange rind and juice and parsley. Mix well.

Place the pastry sheet on a floured board. Place the chicken mixture in the centre of the pastry and, with wet hands, pat the mixture into a neat loaf shape. Brush the loaf with the egg. Wrap the pastry around the loaf to enclose it securely. Turn it over and place it on a baking tray, decorate it with pastry trimmings. Brush the top and sides with egg and bake at 175°C (350°F) for 50 minutes.

Serves 6 to 8.

CHICKEN FILLETS WITH MANGO MAYONNAISE

4 chicken breast fillets

2 cups (500 ml/16 fl oz) chicken stock

1 cup (250 ml/8 fl oz) mayonnaise

2 large mangoes, sliced

2 teaspoons medium curry paste

salt and pepper to taste

2–4 tablespoons fresh cream

watercress sprigs for garnish

Gently poach the chicken fillets in the stock until firm to touch, about 8 minutes. Leave to cool in the stock and drain.

Place the mayonnaise, mango slices, curry paste and salt and pepper in the food processor and blend well. If the mixture is too thick add enough cream to make a coating consistency. Coat the chicken with the sauce and garnish with watercress.

Serves 4.

COLD CRUMBED CUTLETS

10 lamb cutlets, cut thickly

1 cup (60 g/2 oz) fresh white breadcrumbs

2 cloves garlic, crushed

2 teaspoons chopped red chilli

1 teaspoon grated fresh ginger

1 teaspoon chopped fresh thyme

2 teaspoons ground cumin

1 tablespoon castor sugar

flour seasoned with salt and freshly ground pepper

2 eggs, beaten for coating

Trim any excess fat from the cutlets. Mix together the breadcrumbs, garlic, chilli, ginger, thyme, cumin and sugar. Coat the cutlets with the flour, dip them into the egg, and coat both sides with the breadcrumb mixture. Place the coated cutlets in the refrigerator for 30 minutes. Place them on a greased baking tray and bake at 220°C (425°F) for 20 minutes.

Serves 5 to 10.

POTATO TORTILLA

2 large potatoes
2 large onions, peeled and thinly sliced
olive oil for frying
6–8 eggs, depending on size
salt and white pepper to taste

Peel and slice the potatoes evenly and thinly and parboil them for a few minutes, or until they are just tender — do not allow them to break up. Drain the water off the potatoes. Gently fry the onions in about 6 mm (¼ in) of oil until soft but not brown (this recipe fills a 20 x 5 cm/ 8 x 2 in frying pan). Drain the onions and pour the oil back into the pan. Beat the eggs with the salt and pepper. Carefully add the potatoes and onions to the egg mixture and pour it into the frying pan, smoothing the top flat. Cook very slowly until the sides and underneath are just golden and the top is firm. Place under a hot grill to brown.

This dish is best made the day before the picnic. When it has cooled, place it on a serving dish and refrigerate it overnight.

Serves 8.

HOMEMADE MAYONNAISE

1 egg
2 egg yolks
½ teaspoon dry mustard
½ teaspoon salt
¼ teaspoon pepper
2 teaspoons lemon juice or wine vinegar
1 cup (250 ml/8 fl oz) olive oil
1 cup (250 ml/8 fl oz) vegetable oil

In a food processor, blend the eggs and seasonings for 60 seconds. With the food processor still running, add the lemon juice or vinegar and then add the oil, 1 teaspoon at a time, until about half a cup is used (pour in the rest in a thin stream). Refrigerate before serving.

Makes about 3 cups (750 ml/24 fl oz).

WATERCRESS MAYONNAISE

½ cup watercress leaves
1 cup (250 ml/8 fl oz) Homemade Mayonnaise
  (page 117) (bought mayonnaise will do)
1 teaspoon lemon juice

Place the watercress in a food processor and purée until smooth. Add the mayonnaise (homemade or bought) and the lemon juice and mix until thoroughly combined. Serve with Fresh Vegetable Terrine (page 114).

Serves 8.

MESCULIN SALAD

Combine a variety of lettuces, such as oak-leaf, red and green raddicio, arugula, cos and buttercrunch — use whatever is available locally at this time of the year. Add the watercress and nasturtium leaves and any edible flowers, like marigolds, nasturtiums and pansies, that you have available. Toss the lettuces with French (vinaigrette) Dressing (see page 92).

ORANGES IN COINTREAU

8–10 large oranges
1 cup (250 g/8 fl oz) white sugar
½ cup (125 ml/4 fl oz) water
60 ml (2 fl oz) Cointreau or to taste

Using a sharp serrated knife, carefully peel the oranges. Remove all pith. Place the oranges in a shallow serving dish. Select large unblemished pieces of peel and cut them into 7.5-cm x 1-cm (3-in x ½ -in) strips to yield about 1 cup. Place them in a saucepan with the sugar and water and boil for 3 minutes. Cool slightly and add the Cointreau. Arrange a lattice design of peel on top of each orange, and spoon the syrup over. Serve chilled.

Serves 8 to 10.

LIGHT CHRISTMAS CAKE

420 g (14 oz) mixed fruit
125 g (4 oz) unsalted butter
⅓ cup (90 g/3 oz) white sugar
⅓ cup (60 g/2 oz) brown sugar
1 teaspoon mixed spice
½ cup (125 ml/4 fl oz) sherry
½ cup (125 ml/4 fl oz) orange juice
2 eggs
1 cup (125 g/4 oz) plain flour
1 cup (125 g/4 oz) self-raising flour

Line and grease a 17-cm (7-in) square cake tin. Combine the mixed fruit, butter, sugars, spice, sherry and orange juice in a saucepan and simmer for 5 minutes. Put aside to cool.

Beat the eggs lightly and sift the flours. Gradually add the eggs and flour to the fruit mixture. Pour the mixture into the cake tin and bake at 165°C (325°F) for 1¼ to 1½ hours. Turn out and cool on a wire cooling rack. Leave for 24 hours before cutting.

BAKEWELL TARTS

frozen shortcrust pastry, thawed
¼ cup (90 g/3 oz) raspberry jam
60 g (2 oz) butter
¼ cup (60 g/2 oz) white sugar
1 egg
¾ cup (90 g/3 oz) ground almonds
¼ teaspoon almond essence

Roll the pastry out thinly and cut it into 5-cm (2-in) rounds, press them into 12 patty pans. Prick the sides and bottom. Bake at 200°C (400°F) for 5 minutes. Prick the pastry again and fill each pastry case with 1 teaspoon of jam.

Blend the butter and sugar with a fork. Mix in the egg, almonds and almond essence. Spoon the topping onto the jam, covering it completely. Bake for 10 to 12 minutes, or until lightly browned. Remove the tarts immediately from the pans and cool on a wire cooling rack.

Makes 12 tarts.

MOIST GINGERBREAD CAKE

2 cups (250 g/8 oz) plain flour
2 teaspoons cinnamon
¼ teaspoon grated nutmeg
pinch of salt
⅓ cup (60 g/2 oz) pitted dates, chopped
⅓ cup (60 g/2 oz) crystallised ginger, chopped
½ teaspoon black treacle
60 g (2 oz) butter
1 egg
⅓ cup (60 g/2 oz) brown sugar
½ teaspoon bicarbonate of soda
¼ cup (60 ml/2 fl oz) milk

Sift the flour, cinnamon, nutmeg and salt into a large mixing bowl. Stir in the dates and ginger. Soften the treacle and butter in a pan. Beat the egg and add the sugar. Add equal amounts of the two mixtures, alternately, to the sifted dry ingredients until mixed completely. Mix the bicarbonate of soda with the milk and add to the mixture. Pour it into a lined and greased 20-cm (8-in) square cake tin. Bake at 175°C (350°F) for 45 to 50 minutes. Allow the cake to cool in the tin. Remove from tin and wrap it in foil, then put in an airtight container. (This cake will keep for up to 8 weeks.)

PREVIOUS PAGES: *Bakewell Tarts, Moist Gingerbread Cake and Light Christmas Cake.*

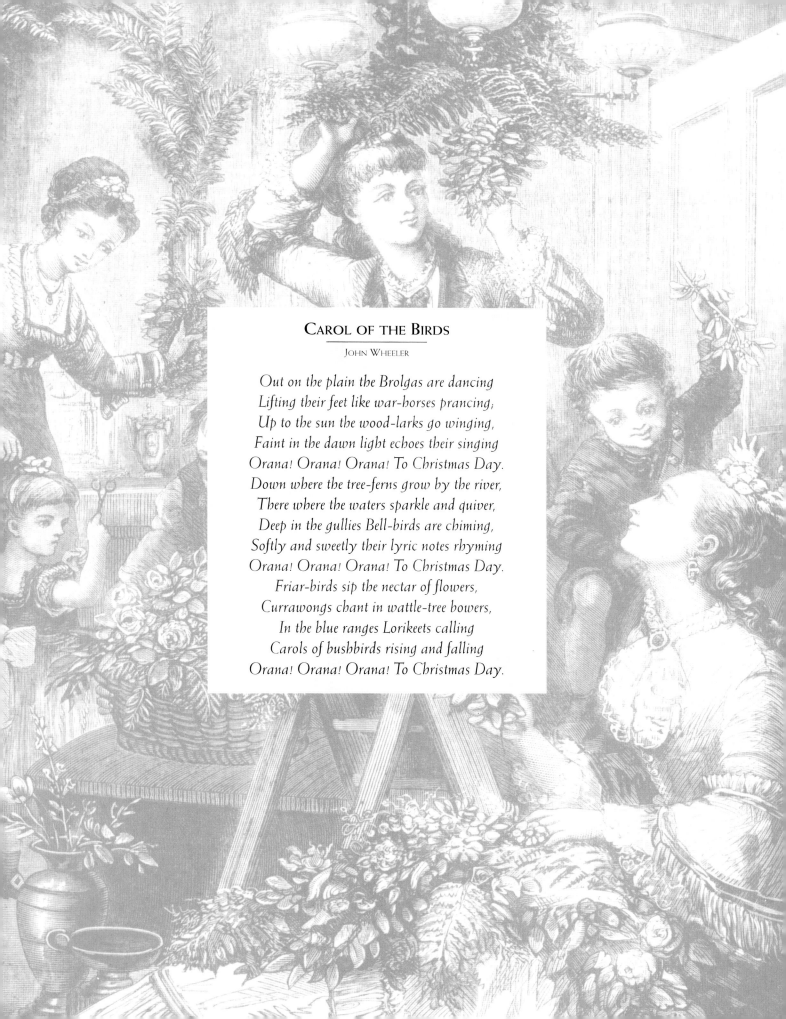

CAROL OF THE BIRDS

John Wheeler

Out on the plain the Brolgas are dancing
Lifting their feet like war-horses prancing;
Up to the sun the wood-larks go winging,
Faint in the dawn light echoes their singing
Orana! Orana! Orana! To Christmas Day.
Down where the tree-ferns grow by the river,
There where the waters sparkle and quiver,
Deep in the gullies Bell-birds are chiming,
Softly and sweetly their lyric notes rhyming
Orana! Orana! Orana! To Christmas Day.
Friar-birds sip the nectar of flowers,
Currawongs chant in wattle-tree bowers,
In the blue ranges Lorikeets calling
Carols of bushbirds rising and falling
Orana! Orana! Orana! To Christmas Day.

Christmas
On the Beach

If you are lucky enough to live near one of Australia's beautiful beaches, then why not take advantage of this and have your Christmas dinner on the beach. Make an effort and take down a portable table and chairs. It is best to head off to the beach after the sun has gone down and the breeze offers relief from what is almost always a very hot Christmas Day. Choose from the menu on page 124.

Christmas on the Beach

Sparkling Kir

Herb damper

Iced cucumber and mint soup

Smoked fish pate

Traditional american glazed ham

Honey marinated
chicken legs

Crusted lamb fillet

Mustard fruits

Tomato ring mould

Potatoes-in-the-skin salad

Vegetable salad with feta cheese and
yoghurt dressing

Summer pudding

Zucchini bread

Apple and almond tart

Boiled fruit cake

Almond shortbread

Suggested Wines

Dry White:
Craneford Springton Rhine Riesling

Light Dry Red:
Meadowbank (Tasmania) Pinot Noir

Sparkling White:
Wirra Wirra 'The Cousins'

SPARKLING KIR

30 ml (1 fl oz) cassis
250 ml (8 fl oz) champagne or sparkling dry white
  wine, chilled
2 slices of halved orange for garnish

Cassis is a liqueur made from macerating blackcurrants in spirit. The popularity of this liqueur has increased with the popularity of Kir, the apéritif made from cassis.

Put the cassis into two chilled apéritif glasses, top them up with the champagne or the sparkling dry white wine. Mix well and garnish with an orange slice.

Serves 2.

HERB DAMPER

¼ cup (30 g/1 oz) self-raising flour
1 teaspoon salt
¼ cup (30 g/1 oz) dried milk powder
¾ cup (155 g/5 oz) bran
3 tablespoons of chopped parsley, oregano, thyme,
  marjoram and rosemary
¾ cup (185 ml/6 fl oz) water
milk for glazing

Sift the flour, salt and milk powder into a large mixing bowl. Stir in the bran and fresh herbs. Add the water and gently mix to make a sticky dough. On a lightly floured board, gently knead the dough and form it into a large ball.

Place the dough on a greased baking tray. Pat it out to about 20 cm (8 in) in diameter. Using a sharp knife, cut wedges into the dough about 1 cm (½ in) deep. Brush with milk and bake at 175°C (350°F) for 25 minutes, or until lightly browned. For the best results serve the damper the same day it is baked.

ICED CUCUMBER AND MINT SOUP

3 medium cucumbers, peeled, seeded and diced
4 spring onions, chopped
2 cups (500 ml/16 fl oz) chicken stock
salt and pepper to taste
30 g (1 oz) butter
2 tablespoons chopped mint or basil
½ cup (125 ml/4 fl oz) sour cream

Place the cucumber in a saucepan with the spring onions, chicken stock, salt and pepper, butter and mint or basil. Cover and simmer until tender. Pour into a food processor and blend until smooth. Strain, cover and chill for a minimum of 3 hours. Stir in the sour cream just before serving. (This soup is even better chilled overnight, and is very easy to make in large quantities.)

Serves 6.

SMOKED FISH PATE

2 smoked mackerel, trout or taylor
250 g (8 oz) cream cheese
250 g (8 oz) butter, softened
juice of 1 small lemon
freshly ground black pepper to taste
fresh or sour cream as needed

Skin the fish and remove all the bones. Break the flesh up into small pieces. Place the fish and all other ingredients in the food processor and blend until smooth. If the mixture is too thick, add a little fresh or sour cream. Pour into a serving bowl, cover and refrigerate until set, or if you wish to turn the pâté out later, pour it into an oiled mould. Serve with Herb Damper (above) or rye bread. (This pâté freezes well.)

Serves 12 to 16.

FOLLOWING PAGES: *Clockwise from the top: Herb Damper; Vegetable Salad with Feta Cheese and Yoghurt Dressing (page 129); Mustard Fruits (page 129); yoghurt; olives; Tomato Ring Mould (page 129); Honey Marinated Chicken Legs (page 128); Crusted Lamb Fillet (page 128); and in the centre of the setting, Iced Cucumber and Mint Soup.*

TRADITIONAL AMERICAN GLAZED HAM

4 kg (8 lb) ham
1 ½ cups (250 g/8 oz) brown sugar
2 teaspoons mustard powder
½ cup (60 g/2 oz) dry breadcrumbs
3 tablespoons malt vinegar or prune juice, white wine or
    ham dripping
whole cloves
pineapple slices for garnish

Unwrap the ham, wipe it with a damp cloth and place it on a rack, in a baking dish. Bake at 165°C (325°F), allow 30 minutes per 500 g (2 lb) for a half ham or 25 minutes per 500 g (2 lb) for a whole ham.

Remove the ham 1 hour before it is due to come out of the oven. Remove the rind, except for a collar around the shank bone. Cut diagonal slashes across the fat side of the ham to make diamond shapes.

Combine the remaining ingredients together, except the cloves and pineapple. Brush the top (fat side) of the ham with the mixture and stud the centre of each diamond with a clove. Return the ham to the oven for 45 minutes. Increase the temperature to 200°C (400°F) and bake for a further 15 minutes. Heat the pineapple slices in the baking dish with the ham for the last 15 minutes. Garnish the ham with the heated pineapple. Serve warm or cold, with Mustard Fruits).

Serves about 24.

HONEY MARINATED CHICKEN LEGS

2 tablespoons peanut or sunflower oil
¼ cup (60 ml/2 fl oz) light soy sauce
1 clove garlic, crushed
¼ cup (60 ml/2 fl oz) honey
1 tablespoon dry sherry
12 chicken drumsticks

Combine the oil, soy sauce, garlic, honey and sherry in a screw-top jar. Shake well to combine. Pour the mixture over the drumsticks. Cover and allow to marinate overnight in the refrigerator.

Bake the chicken legs, in a single layer and in the marinade, at 190°C (375°F) for 45 to 50 minutes or until tender, occasionally baste with the marinade during cooking. Allow them to cool in the liquid, serve chilled.

Serves 6 to 12.

CRUSTED LAMB FILLET

2 tablespoons olive oil
2 cloves garlic, peeled and halved
½ teaspoon crushed rosemary leaves
salt and freshly ground pepper to taste
1 leg of lamb, boned and rolled
45 g (1 ½ oz) dry breadcrumbs
4 tablespoons finely chopped parsley
melted butter, if necessary

Place the olive oil, garlic and rosemary into a food processor and blend to a paste. Add the salt and pepper. Spread the garlic paste over the lamb and leave it for about 3 hours. Cook the lamb at 150°C (300°F), allow 25 minutes per 500 g (1 lb).

Mix the breadcrumbs and parsley together. About 30 minutes before the meat is due to come out of the oven, spoon off the lamb juices and mix with the breadcrumbs and parsley until it forms a paste. If necessary, add a little butter to make the paste a spreading consistency. Spread the paste over the lamb and return it to the oven for a further 30 minutes to brown the crust. .

Serves 6 to 8.

MUSTARD FRUITS

1 kg (2 lb) fresh fruit in season
500 g (1 lb) glace fruits
2½ cups (625 g/1¼ lb) white sugar
⅓ cup (90 ml/3 fl oz) water
⅓ cup (90 ml/3 fl oz) lemon juice
½ cup (125 ml/4 fl oz) red wine vinegar
2 tablespoons prepared mustard
2 cloves garlic, crushed

Peel, core and thickly slice the fresh and glacé fruits of your choice and place them in a mixing bowl (any combination of fresh and glacé fruits may be used). Combine the sugar, water, lemon juice and red wine vinegar in a large, non-aluminium pan. Stir over a medium heat until the sugar is dissolved. Bring to the boil and cook for 5 minutes. Add the prepared mustard and garlic cloves. Stir in the fruits, bring to the boil again and simmer for 5 minutes. Pack into hot, sterilised jars (see page 48).

Mustard fruits are served as an accompaniment to meat. They may be served hot or cold and should be stored for at least 1 week before using. Once opened, store in the refrigerator.

TOMATO RING MOULD

1 cup (250 ml/8 fl oz) tomato purée
1 cup (250 ml/8 fl oz) water
2 teaspoons powdered gelatine in 3 tablespoons water
4 tablespoons white sugar
1 white onion, finely chopped
3 hard-boiled eggs, sliced into rings
1 cup (250 g/8 oz) chopped celery
salt and pepper to taste
cooked asparagus, for serving
black olives, for garnish

Heat the tomato purée and water. Add the gelatine and sugar and stir until dissolved. Cool. Add the onion, eggs, celery and salt and pepper. Pour into a lightly oiled mould and refrigerate until set. Fill the centre with asparagus. Garnish.

Serves 8 to 12.

POTATOES-IN-THE-SKIN SALAD

Dressing
1 cup (250 ml/8 fl oz) mayonnaise
2 cups (500 ml/16 fl oz) sour cream
1 teaspoon mustard powder

Salad
2 kg (4 lb) small new potatoes
3 rashers lean bacon
3 tablespoons shredded mint

Make the dressing: put all ingredients together in a screw-top jar, tighten the lid and shake the jar to mix the ingredients.

Make the salad: boil the potatoes in their skins until they are just tender — don't overcook them. Drain the potatoes and cool. Cut them into halves or quarters. Chop, fry and drain the bacon. Fold the potatoes, bacon and mint into the dressing. (Shred the mint just before combining it with the salad.)

Serves 16 to 24.

VEGETABLE SALAD WITH FETA CHEESE AND YOGHURT DRESSING

1 cup (250 ml/8 fl oz) natural yoghurt
2 tablespoons safflower oil
1 tablespoon lemon juice
salt and freshly ground black pepper to taste
185 g (6 oz) feta cheese, cubed
250 g (8 oz) green beans, trimmed, parboiled
    and cooled
250 g (8 oz) carrots, sliced diagonally, parboiled
    and cooled
250 g (8 oz) zucchini, sliced diagonally, parboiled
    and cooled
chopped parsley or watercress for garnish

Mix the yoghurt, oil, lemon juice and salt and pepper in a food processor and chill in the refrigerator. To serve, toss the cheese with the vegetables and pour the dressing over. Garnish with the parsley or watercress.

Serves 8.

SUMMER PUDDING

10 thick slices white bread, crusts removed
250 g (8 oz) raspberries
250 g (8 oz) strawberries
250 g (8 oz) redcurrants
¾ cup (185 g/6 oz) castor sugar
1 cup (250 ml/8 fl oz) water
fresh cream and extra berries for decoration

Line a 4-cup pudding basin with overlapping slices of bread, reserving several slices for the top. Combine the berries, sugar and water in a saucepan and cook gently until the sugar is dissolved. Bring to the boil and simmer for 3 minutes. Fill the mould with the fruit and most of the syrup. Cover with the remaining bread slices and pour the reserved syrup over it. Place a flat plate or saucer on top of the bread and place a weight on the plate to weigh down the pudding. Refrigerate overnight.

ZUCCHINI BREAD

3 cups (375 g/12 oz) wholemeal flour
1 cup (250 ml/8 fl oz) honey
1 teaspoon salt
1 teaspoon ground cinnamon
1 teaspoon bicarbonate of soda
½ teaspoon baking powder
2 eggs, beaten
1 cup (250 ml/8 fl oz) safflower oil
2 teaspoons vanilla essence
2 cups (185 g/6 oz) grated zucchini

Combine the flour, honey, salt and cinnamon in a large mixing bowl. Add the remaining ingredients and mix thoroughly. Pour into a greased and floured loaf tin. Bake at 175°C (350°F) for 1 hour, or until the bread is cooked.

RIGHT: *Summer Pudding.*
BELOW: *Potatoes-in-the-skin Salad (page 129).*

APPLE AND ALMOND TART

1 packet frozen shortcrust pastry, thawed

200 g (7 oz) marzipan roll, coarsely grated

90 g (3 oz) unsalted butter or margarine

¼ cup (125 g/4 oz) castor sugar

2 teaspoons lemon juice

4 large cooking apples

2 large egg whites

pinch of salt

beaten egg for glazing

Roll out two-thirds of the pastry to fit a 23-cm (9-in) round flan tin. Trim the edges. Prick the pastry with a fork. Spread the marzipan into the pastry case. Beat together the butter or margarine, sugar and lemon juice until creamy. Peel and core the apples and grate them into the creamed mixture. Add the salt to the egg whites and whisk them until stiff. Fold the egg into the apple mixture and spread evenly over the marzipan. Roll out the remaining pastry and, using a sharp knife or pastry wheel, cut 6 strips of pastry about 2 cm (1 in) wide. Arrange lattice-fashion over the filling. Brush over the top of the pastry with the beaten egg. Bake at 200°C (400°F) until cooked and browned, about 35 to 40 minutes.

Serves 8.

BOILED FRUIT CAKE

500 g (1 lb) mixed dried fruit

1 cup (250 g/8 oz) white sugar

2 teaspoons mixed spice

1 teaspoon bicarbonate of soda

125 g (4 oz) butter

1 cup (250 ml/8 fl oz) water

1 large egg, lightly beaten

2 cups (250 g/8 oz) self-raising flour

almonds, walnuts or pecans and glacé cherries for
   decoration

Place the fruit, sugar, mixed spice, bicarbonate of soda, butter and water into a saucepan and bring to the boil. Simmer for 5 minutes. Allow to cool. Stir in the egg and flour. Pour the mixture into a lined and greased cake or loaf tin and bake at 175°C (350°F) for 1 to 1½ hours. Turn out and cool on a wire cooling rack. Serve decorated with roasted almonds, walnuts or pecans and glacé cherries.

ALMOND SHORTBREAD

2 cups (250 g/8 oz) plain flour

¼ cup (60 g/2 oz) icing sugar

1 tablespoon ground rice

½ cup (60 g/2 oz) ground almonds

250 g (8 oz) butter

castor sugar for dusting

Sift the flour, icing sugar, ground rice and almonds into a mixing bowl. Rub the butter in with your fingertips until the mixture is smooth. Roll out onto a lightly floured board to about 6 mm (¼ in). Cut it into rounds and gently press with a wooden shortbread mould. Dust with castor sugar and place on an ungreased baking tray. Bake at 165°C (325°F) for 20 minutes. Remove from the oven and allow to cool on a wire cooling rack to prevent the undersides from becoming soggy.

If you do not have a mould, cut the shortbread into 5-cm (2-in) rounds, pinch the edges with your fingertips and bake as above. Or divide the mixture into 2 portions and roll each to make 2 x 18-cm (7-in) circles. With a knife, mark 8 sections and pinch the edges with your fingertips. Bake for 45 minutes.

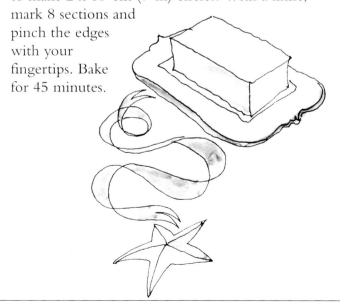

A FESTIVE POEM

RHYLL MCMASTER

Balanced precariously on the backs of chairs
tacking awkwardly strung together Christmas cards
to the pelmet,
with thumbs feeling like pressed-out putty
and the kids scrambling,
squealing 'We can touch the ceiling!'
The time of the year we damn auntie
for her 'thought that counts' gifts of gussies
untimely opened;
and brightly choke
our stunted sheoak with tangled lights
only to see them bad-connectedly go
phftt.
Time we make the drunken fruit mince
and rub flour into the calicoed pudding
knowing all the while we'll be too hot to eat it
tomorrow....
sitting on the beach
with sandflies on our silver hair-bleached arms
we say listlessly,
'It doesn't really feel Christmassy.'

BARBECUED TUNA STEAKS WITH TOMATO TAPENADE

Tuna
12 small tuna steaks
herbed lemon pepper to taste
juice of ½ lemon
olive oil
melted butter

Tomato Tapenade
1 cup (250 g/8 oz) sun-dried tomatoes in oil, drained
80 ml (2½ fl oz) oil from tomatoes
4 large cloves garlic, crushed
1 small red onion, chopped
125 ml (4 fl oz) water
1 tablespoon red wine vinegar
2 tablespoons olive oil

Pat the tuna dry and sprinkle it with the lemon pepper and lemon juice. Place the fish on a hot barbecue plate brushed with oil and butter. Cook each side for 2 to 3 minutes, or until just cooked, turning carefully.

Make the tapenade: place the sun-dried tomatoes, oil from the tomatoes, garlic and onion in a saucepan. Cover and sauté gently until the onion is transparent. Allow the mixture to cool slightly and, in a food processor, purée till smooth. Add the water, vinegar and olive oil and mix well. Serve with the tuna.

Serves 12.

ASPARAGUS

500 g (16 oz) asparagus spears
salted water
1 teaspoon butter

Trim off the tough end of each asparagus stalk. In a large frying pan or saucepan, bring to the boil about 6 cm (2½ in) of salted water and butter. Lay the asparagus flat in the pan and cook, uncovered, for about five minutes, or until tender but still crisp. Remove the asparagus from the pan and place it into cold water for a few minutes. Remove and drain well before serving. Serve with Bearnaise Sauce.

BEARNAISE SAUCE

2 egg yolks
2 tablespoons fresh cream
1 tablespoon tarragon vinegar
pinch of cayenne
125 g (4 oz) butter
1 teaspoon finely chopped fresh tarragon
½ teaspoon finely chopped fresh parsley
½ teaspoon snipped fresh chives

In the top of a double saucepan over gently boiling water, whisk together the egg yolks, cream, vinegar and cayenne. Stir continuously until the mixture thickens. Gradually add small pieces of butter, beating all the time (or the mixture will separate). When the sauce is the consistency of thick custard, remove from the heat and stir in the herbs. Serve Bearnaise Sauce hot or cold, with freshly cooked asparagus spears.

Serves 4 to 6.

Some sauces, like bearnaise, can be a little nerve-racking to make at the last minute. Try making it shortly before it is needed and pour it into a thermos until you are ready to use it.

TOMATO, BASIL AND BOCCONCINI SALAD

tomatoes, thinly sliced
whole basil leaves
bocconcini cheese, thinly sliced
French (vinaigrette) Dressing (page 92)
basil for garnish

Arrange the tomatoes in a circle around a
serving platter. Arrange the individual basil leaves
on the tomatoes and the bocconcini slices on the
basil. Continue alternating layers, working in to
the centre until the platter is completed. Drizzle
with French dressing and garnish the centre with
a small bunch of basil before serving.

ROSY RICE SALAD

1 cup (155 g/5 oz) long-grain rice, cooked, drained
   and cooled
½ small red onion, thinly sliced
½ red sweet pepper (capsicum), chopped and deseeded
250 g (8 oz) tomatoes, chopped
3 tablespoons chopped parsley
salt and pepper to taste
2 cloves garlic, crushed
250 ml (8 fl oz) French (vinaigrette) Dressing (page 92)

Mix the rice, red onion, sweet pepper, tomatoes
and parsley together in a salad bowl with the salt
and pepper. Mix the garlic with the dressing in a
screw-top jar and add just before serving.

Serves 8 to 12.

ALMOND BREAD

4 egg whites
pinch of salt
125 g (4 oz) castor sugar
125 g (4 oz) plain flour, sifted
125 g (4 oz) unblanched almonds
8 drops almond essence

Whisk the egg whites with the salt until stiff.
Gradually add the sugar, whisking continuously.
Fold in the sifted flour and gently stir in the
almonds and almond essence.
Pour into a greased loaf tin and bake at 180°C
(350°F) for 35 minutes. When cool, this bread
may be wrapped and deep frozen. When needed,
thaw and cut into wafer thin slices. Place on a
baking tray until heated through.

MANGOES AND PEACHES IN CHAMPAGNE

1 kg (2 lb) mangoes, peeled, stoned and sliced
1 kg (2 lb) peaches, peeled, stoned and sliced
1 large bunch mint, finely chopped
½ cup (125 g/4 oz) castor sugar
½ bottle champagne or sparkling white wine
mint leaves and sugared berries, for decoration

Using a tall glass container, place a 2-cm (¾-in)
layer of mangoes on the bottom, cover with a
layer of peaches and a layer of mint, then sprinkle
with castor sugar and a little champagne.
Continue until all the fruit, mint, sugar and
champagne is used, finishing with a layer of fruit.
Cover and refrigerate for 1 to 3 days.
Decorate with mint sprigs and sugared berries.

Serves about 24 to 32.

> *To sugar berries, take blueberries, raspberries,*
> *blackcurrants or redcurrants, and dip them in*
> *lightly whisked egg white, then coat them with*
> *castor sugar and leave them to dry on a wire*
> *cooling rack. Use the berries on the same day*
> *that they are prepared.*

STRAWBERRY OR RASPBERRY SORBET

250 g (8 oz) strawberries, or fresh or frozen raspberries
½ cup (125 ml/4 fl oz) water
4 tablespoons castor sugar
1 tablespoon lemon juice

Prepare the fruit according to your choice of berry — wash and hull the strawberries or pick over and clean the raspberries, as necessary.
Gently boil the water and sugar together for 5 minutes. Cool. Purée the berries and strain. Combine the purée and lemon juice with the cooled syrup. Pour the mixture into a jug and refrigerate until very cold.
Transfer the mixture to an ice-cream churn and mix for 20 minutes, or as directed for your machine. Freeze until served.

Serves 4 to 6.

LEMON SORBET

250 g (8 oz) loaf sugar
500 ml (16 fl oz) water
250 ml (8 fl oz) lemon juice
2 egg whites
crystallised flowers, for serving

Combine the sugar and water in a saucepan. Stir the mixture until the sugar has dissolved. Bring to the boil and boil for 10 minutes. Strain, pour into a jug and chill. Add the lemon juice. Whisk the egg whites until stiff and carefully fold them into the lemon mixture.
Transfer the mixture to an ice-cream churn and mix for 20 minutes, or as directed for your machine. Freeze until served.

Serves 8 to 12.

RIGHT: *Mangoes and Peaches in Champagne (page 141) and Strawberry, Lemon and Kiwi Fruit Sorbet.*

KIWI FRUIT SORBET

250 g (8 oz) castor sugar
200 ml (6½ fl oz) water
6 large ripe kiwi fruit, to make 2 cups (500 ml/16 fl oz) of purée
2 tablespoons lemon juice
1 tablespoon orange juice
crystallised flowers, for serving

Boil the sugar and water together gently for 5 minutes. Cool. Peel the kiwi fruit and purée. Strain well to remove black seeds. Combine the purée, lemon and orange juice and cooled syrup. Pour into a jug and refrigerate until very cold.
Transfer the mixture to an ice-cream churn and mix for 20 minutes, or as directed for your machine. Freeze until served.

Serves 8 to 12.

WALNUT CAKE

Syrup
300 g (10 oz) white sugar
150 ml (5 fl oz) water
2 tablespoons brandy
juice of ½ lemon

Cake
5 eggs, separated
100 g (3½ oz) castor sugar
4 tablespoons breadcrumbs
120 g (4 oz) walnuts, coarsely ground
grated rind of 1 lemon
1 teaspoon ground cinnamon
2 tablespoons brandy

Make the syrup: boil the sugar and water until fairly thick. Stir in the brandy and lemon juice.
Make the cake: beat the egg yolks and sugar. Add the breadcrumbs, walnuts, rind, cinnamon and brandy. Whisk the egg whites until stiff and fold them into the mixture. Pour the mixture into a lined and buttered round cake tin. Bake at 180°C (350°F) for about 1 hour. Cool the cake slightly in the tin and pour the hot syrup over it.

PEACH FRUIT CAKE

1¾ cups (200 g/7 oz) plain flour
½ cup (125 g/4 oz) brown sugar
½ teaspoon bicarbonate of soda
½ teaspoon ground cinnamon
¼ teaspoon ground cloves
1 cup (250 g/8 oz) mixed candied fruits
½ cup (125 g/4 oz) chopped walnuts
½ cup (125 g/4 oz) sultanas
250 g (8 oz) fresh peaches, drained and chopped
200-g (7½-oz) can sweetened condensed milk
½ cup (125 g/4 oz) fruit mincemeat
½ cup (125 ml/4 fl oz) apricot brandy

Sift the flour, brown sugar, bicarbonate of soda, cinnamon and cloves together into a mixing bowl. Stir in the candied fruits, nuts and sultanas. Add the peaches, condensed milk, fruit mincemeat and ¼ cup (60 ml/2 fl oz) brandy. Stir well. Turn the mixture into a prepared cake tin and bake for about 1½ hours at 150°C (300°F), or until cooked. Cool the cake in the tin, run a knife around the edges and invert onto a wire cooling rack.

Soak a piece of cheesecloth in the remaining brandy and wrap the cake in it, then wrap it in aluminium foil. Store in a cool place.

TRADITIONAL ENGLISH CHRISTMAS CAKE

1 kg (2 lb) mixed dried fruit
½ cup (125 ml/2 oz) brandy
4 tablespoons sherry
4 tablespoons rum
250 g (8 oz) unsalted butter
125 g (4 oz) brown sugar
125 g (4 oz) white sugar
4 x 60 g (2 oz) eggs
250 g (8 oz) plain flour
60 g (2 oz) self-raising flour
2 teaspoons mixed spice
1 tablespoon apricot jam
1 tablespoon currants
125 g (4 oz) glacé cherries
60 g (2 oz) chopped figs or prunes
60 g (2 oz) chopped pineapple
30 g (1 oz) chopped almonds
30 g (1 oz) chopped walnuts
2 teaspoons parisienne essence

Soak the mixed fruit overnight in the brandy, sherry and rum. Grease and line a 20-cm (8-in) round or square tin with one layer of brown paper and two layers of foil or greaseproof paper. Allow the paper to come about 4–5 cm (1½–2 in) above the top of the tin.

Cream together the butter and the sugars. Add the eggs, one at a time, and beat well. Sieve the flours and mixed spice. Add half the flour and spice, and half the fruit and liquor. Mix well, add the remaining flour and fruit and other ingredients, and some more liquor if necessary. Carefully add the parisienne essence to darken the cake. Mix thoroughly.

Place the mixture in the prepared cake tin. Cover the top shelf of the oven with brown paper. Place the cake about 5 cm (2 in) from the bottom of a 160°C (320°F) oven and cook for half an hour. Reduce the oven temperature to 150°C (300°F) and cook for a further 3½ to 4 hours. Test with a skewer.

Remove the cake from the tin and wrap it in a teatowel and several layers of newspaper. Set it aside for 2 to 3 days or more before icing.

Icing the Cake

Traditionally the Christmas cake is first brushed with apricot glaze or lightly whisked egg white, followed by a layer of almond paste and then covered with royal icing.

First, prepare the surface of the cake. Any fruit holes or paper creases should be filled with almond paste and then smoothed out with a palette knife until you have a completely level surface. Any unevenness must be cut away to ensure the cake stands flat and level, with the sides equal in height. Place the cake on greaseproof paper before icing. The entire surface of the cake should now be brushed lightly with egg white or apricot glaze. If the jam is too thick, break it down with water, bring to the boil and cool prior to using. This prevents fermentation which will cause patches to show through.

Roll the almond paste out on a board or marble slab dusted with icing sugar. Once a size has been reached that will provide a thick cover, the paste should be placed onto the cake, with the help of a rolling pin. With cupped hands, mould the paste to the cake. Trim away any excess around the base. Allow to dry for at least 24 hours.

When the cake is finished, secure it to a covered board with a layer of royal icing. If you are icing with royal icing, spread it on smoothly, using a palette knife, or spread on and drag up quickly to make it resemble snow.

Apricot Glaze

250 g (8 oz) apricot jam
juice of half a small lemon
2 tablespoons of water

Bring all ingredients slowly to the boil. Simmer for 5 minutes and strain. Boil for another 5 minutes. Cool and store in a sterilised jar. No additional water will be necessary if the glaze is smooth and free from chunks of fruit.

Almond Paste

250 g (8 oz) ground almonds
180 g (6 oz) castor sugar
125 g (4 oz) pure icing sugar, finely sifted
1 egg
1 tablespoon lemon juice
1 tablespoon brandy or sherry
½ teaspoon vanilla essence
3 drops almond essence
2 teaspoons orange flower water, extra sherry
or lemon juice

Combine the almonds, castor sugar and icing sugar. Whisk together the egg, lemon juice, liquor, essences and orange flower water. Add the liquid to the almond mixture and pound lightly to release the natural oil. Knead the mixture until smooth.

Royal Icing

1 egg white, at room temperature
500 g (1 lb) icing sugar, very finely sifted
2 drops acetic acid

Beat the egg white with 1 tablespoon of icing sugar until the sugar is completely dissolved. Add sugar to the mixture until it is shiny and smooth, with the consistency of golden syrup. To give a free-flowing icing, add the acetic acid . Beat the mixture well. Add icing sugar in quantities of half a tablespoon at a time. Beat well between each addition, until the mixture is firm enough to hold a peak that stands firm and tapered.

The royal icing is now ready for use and must be covered with a damp cloth to prevent a crust forming. It is not advisable to beat this icing with an electric mixer as it causes air to enter and so produces a false volume. This icing may be stored in the refrigerator for 1 to 2 days.

This recipe produces enough icing for the top of the cake only; triple the quantity if you are icing the sides of the cake as well.

Formal CHRISTMAS DINNER

Christmas is the perfect time of the year to make an extra effort and sit down to a formal dinner. Take time to decorate your table using ideas in chapters 1 and 2 and choose your courses from the menu on page 148.

FORMAL CHRISTMAS DINNER

CHAMPAGNE COCKTAIL PUNCH

DECORATIVE ICE BOWL

KIDS' PINEAPPLE PUNCH

DEVILLED ALMONDS

CHEESY BISCUITS

TOMATO AND BASIL SOUP

SALMON PATE

DAMPER ROLLS

ROAST GOOSE WITH APPLE STUFFING

CROWN ROAST OF LAMB WITH APPLEMINT
STUFFING

BEAN BUNDLES

NEW POTATOES WITH DILL

CARAMELISED CARROTS

BROCCOLI AND CAULIFLOWER TREE

CHRISTMAS PLUM PUDDING
ICE-CREAM

CHRISTMAS CONFECTION CAKE

MINCE PIES

FROSTED GRAPES

BRANDY BUTTER OR HARD SAUCE

CRYSTALLISED FLOWERS

SUGGESTED WINES

Fine Sherry to have with soup:
Lindemans Solera RP 10

Dry Red:
Bests Great Western Cabernet Sauvignon

Dessert Wine:
Bullers Classic Rutherglen Muscat

CHAMPAGNE COCKTAIL PUNCH

½ cup (125 ml/4 fl oz) brandy
½ cup (125 ml/4 fl oz) Curacao
½ cup (125 ml/ 4 fl oz) sherry
3 bottles of champagne, chilled
crushed ice
grapes
mint or borage sprigs
geranium flower petals

Place all liquid ingredients in a large punch bowl, and mix with crushed ice. Decorate with grapes, mint or borage sprigs and geranium petals. Serve in tall glasses.

Makes about 20 glasses.

DECORATIVE ICE BOWL

8.5 cm (3¼ in) tall jam jar
16 x 9 cm (6¼ x 3½ in) glass bowl
matching 21 x 11 cm (8¼ x 4¼ in) glass bowl
clear tape
non-poisonous plant or flower material
thin wire

Invert the jar and in the smaller bowl and place the bowls inside each other. Pour water between the two bowls until the water comes to 1 cm (½ in) below the rim. Fill the jar with water (this will keep the rims level). Hold the bowls and the jar in place with tape.

🦋 Select plant material and slip it between the two bowls, prodding into place with the wire. Wedge any large leaves or flowers toward the base of the bowls. Freeze overnight.

🦋 Remove the tape and the jar, pour cold water into the small bowl. Dip the outer bowl in cold water (warm water will cause ice to crack) to gradually separate the bowls to leave an ice bowl.

🦋 Place the ice bowl on a plate and use it immediately or store it in the freezer.

If you plan to serve drinks from the bowl, freeze small flowers or pieces of fruit in ice cubes to float in your punch.

KIDS' PINEAPPLE PUNCH

3 cups (750 ml/24 fl oz) strong tea, strained
¾ cup (185 ml/6 fl oz) lemon juice
2 cups (500 ml/16 fl oz) pineapple juice
1 cup (250 ml/8 fl oz) fresh orange juice
1 cup (250 g/8 oz) white sugar
2 x 1.25 litre (2 pint) bottles lemonade, chilled
1 x 1.25 litre (2 pint) bottle ginger ale, chilled
lemon slices

In a large bowl, combine the tea with the fruit juices and sugar and chill in the refrigerator. Just before serving, add the chilled lemonade, ginger ale and ice. Decorate each glass with half a slice of lemon.

Makes about 20 glasses.

DEVILLED ALMONDS

¼ cup (60 ml/2 fl oz) oil
250 g (8 oz) blanched almonds
salt to taste
cayenne pepper or chilli powder to taste

Heat the oil in a heavy based frying pan and, stirring occasionally, fry the almonds until they are lightly browned all over. Drain the almonds on kitchen paper towels. Sprinkle the almonds with salt and cayenne or chilli powder, shaking to completely coat the nuts. Store them in an airtight container.

Serves 8 to 12.

PREVIOUS PAGES: *Left to right: Broccoli and Cauliflower Tree (page 154), New Potatoes with Dill (page 153), Crown Roast of Lamb with Applemint Stuffing (page 153) and Caramelised Carrots (page 153).*

CHEESY BISCUITS

500 g (16 oz) butter
500 g (16 oz) plain flour
500 g (16 oz) sharp Cheddar cheese, grated
2 egg yolks
rock salt, walnuts and smoked almonds, grated for
    topping
Parmesan cheese

Using an electric mixer with a dough hook, mix the butter, flour, Cheddar cheese and egg yolks to a stiff dough. Wrap it in greaseproof paper and chill for 30 minutes.

Roll out the dough on a lightly floured board and cut it into small circles, squares or diamonds. Decorate each shape with a topping and roll them in Parmesan cheese. Place them on a greased baking tray and bake at 180°C (350°F) for 8 to 10 minutes.

Cool and store in an airtight container. Serve with drinks.

TOMATO AND BASIL SOUP

16 vine-ripened tomatoes, roughly chopped
1 small onion, peeled and sliced
1 tablespoon tomato purée
1 medium-sized can chicken consommé
2 tablespoons chopped basil
salt and pepper to taste
150 ml (5 fl oz) sour cream
fresh basil leaves, to garnish

In a food processor, blend the tomatoes with the onion, tomato purée, chicken consommé and basil until smooth. Sieve the mixture into a saucepan and gently heat. Add the salt and pepper and chill for at least 2 hours.

Serve chilled with a spoonful of sour cream in each portion, topped with a few basil leaves.

Serves 8 to 12.

RIGHT: *Tomato and Basil Soup.*
BELOW: *Decorative Ice Bowl (page 149).*

SALMON PATE

500 g (16 oz) fresh salmon
1 cup (250 ml/8 fl oz) sherry
salt and pepper
1 spring onion, finely chopped
1 bay leaf
1 cup (125 g/4 oz) fresh white breadcrumbs, soaked
   in milk
2 egg yolks
125 g (4 oz) butter, softened
pinch of ground mace
flour and water, for a paste

Cut two-thirds of the salmon into strips.
Marinate in sherry with salt and pepper, spring
onion and bay leaf. Mix the remaining salmon in
a food processor with the breadcrumbs, egg yolks,
butter and mace.

Butter a loaf tin and place a layer of the
salmon forcemeat on the bottom. Add a layer of
the marinated salmon, removing the bay leaf but
allowing some sherry to go in the tin. Alternate
the layers, finishing with salmon forcemeat on the
top. Cover and seal with a paste made from the
flour and water.

Place the tin in a shallow bath of water and
cook at 150°C (300°F) for 2 hours. Allow to cool
before serving.

DAMPER ROLLS

Follow the recipe for Australian Damper (see
page 89), and divide the mixture into 12 to 14
equal-sized rolls. Place them on a greased baking
tray and bake at 220°C (430°F)
for about 15 minutes, or until the rolls sound
hollow when tapped.

Makes 12 to 14.

ROAST GOOSE WITH APPLE STUFFING

1 x 4½-kg (10-lb) young goose, with giblets

Apple Stuffing
goose giblets
50 g (8 oz) seedless raisins
3¼ cups (410 ml/13 fl oz) boiling water
2½ cups (155 g/5 oz) fresh white breadcrumbs
3 green apples, peeled, cored and chopped
60 g (2 oz) almonds, chopped
3 tablespoons chopped fresh parsley
salt and pepper to taste
2 tablespoons chopped fresh marjoram or 1 teaspoon
   dried marjoram
30 g (1 oz) butter
1 small onion, finely chopped

In a small saucepan, cover the heart and gizzard
(giblets) of the goose with cold water and gently
simmer for 40 minutes, or until tender. Chop
the heart and chop the flesh from the gizzard
bone. Soak the raisins in boiling water until
plump, then drain.

In a large mixing bowl, combine the
breadcrumbs, chopped giblets, raisins, apples,
almonds, parsley and salt and pepper. In a frying
pan, melt the butter, add the onions and cook
them until translucent. Add the chopped goose
liver and cook until lightly browned. Add the
onions and liver to the breadcrumbs mixture and
mix well.

Wash the goose in cold water and pat it dry
inside and out. Sprinkle the inside of the goose
with marjoram. Truss the wings, fill the body
cavity with stuffing and secure the opening with
skewers; place the goose on a roasting rack in a
baking dish. Prick the skin on the thighs and back
in a couple of places with a skewer or sharp knife.
Cook, in a hot oven (230°C/450°F), for
10 minutes. Reduce the heat to 180°C (350°F)
and continue cooking for 3 hours, or until the
juices run clear from the thigh. (Do not baste as
goose has a lot of fat.) Rest for 15 minutes in the
oven with the door ajar before carving.

Serves 8 to 10.

CROWN ROAST OF LAMB WITH APPLEMINT STUFFING

1 crown roast of lamb, 18 to 20 chops
olive oil
1 cup (250 ml/8 fl oz) cider, for basting

Applemint Stuffing
2 cups (120 g/4 oz) fresh white breadcrumbs
1 cup (125 g/4 oz) finely chopped tart apple
2 teaspoons chopped mint
pinch each of salt and paprika
1 egg
2 teaspoons lemon juice
milk, optional

Rub the outside of the roast with a little oil and cover the bone tips with bacon or foil to prevent them burning. Combine all the stuffing ingredients — if the mixture becomes too dry, moisten it with a little milk. Place the stuffing in the centre of the crown roast. For pink lamb, bake at 190°C (375°F) for 50 minutes, basting occasionally with cider. Cook longer if well-cooked lamb is preferred.

When cooked, remove foil or bacon and place a cutlet frill on each bone. Make a gravy from the pan juices and serve hot.

Serves 6 to 8.

BEAN BUNDLES

French or snake beans
long thin strips of red sweet pepper (capsicum)

Top, tail and cut the beans to equal lengths. Boil in salted water until just tender. Remove the beans from the water, add strips of sweet pepper to the boiling water and leave for one to two minutes to soften. Arrange the beans in bundles and tie with sweet pepper strips.

Variation on New Potatoes with Dill

Boil the potatoes until just tender, drain well and chop roughly. Finely chop 3 tablespoons of spring onions. Combine with dill, 150 ml (5 fl oz) sour cream, 1 tablespoon French mustard and 1 teaspoon vinegar, mix well. Add this mixture to the potatoes. Toss carefully and season to taste. Serve warm or cold.

NEW POTATOES WITH DILL

2 kg (4 lb) small new potatoes
60–125 g (2–4 oz) butter
2 tablespoons chopped fresh dill

Boil the potatoes, in their jackets, until tender. Drain and add the butter while still warm. Toss, add the chopped dill and serve.

CARAMELISED CARROTS

carrots, sliced
brown sugar
butter

Cook the carrots until tender and drain. Heat the brown sugar and butter until caramelised and toss through carrots.

BROCCOLI AND CAULIFLOWER TREE

2 kg (4 lb) broccoli, trimmed to serve-size florets

2 kg (4 lb) cauliflower

salt, milk and water for cooking

tiny cherry tomatoes

Cook the broccoli in boiling water until tender but still crisp, for about 5 minutes. Remove the core from the cauliflower and cut the florets the same size as the broccoli. Cook in salted half-milk, half-water until tender but still crisp, about 5 minutes. Remove the broccoli and cauliflower with a slotted spoon and drop them into ice-cold water. Drain and pat dry.

🥄 Take a deep round bowl and, starting at the centre, place alternate circles of vegetable florets, sideways with the stalks facing inwards. Cover the sides of the bowl. Continue layering, fitting the vegetables as close together as possible, making sure the centre is well packed.

🥄 Place a plate over the vegetables and weigh it down. Refrigerate overnight.

🥄 Invert the bowl and, holding the plate, drain off any excess liquid. Turn upside down onto a serving platter. Serve with French (vinaigrette) Dressing (page 92) and decorate with tomatoes.

Serves 8 to 10.

RIGHT: *Clockwise from the top, Mince Pies (page 156), Frosted Grapes (page 156), Christmas Plum Pudding Ice-cream, Christmas Confection Cake (page 156) and Homemade Chocolates (page 58).*
BELOW: *Crown Roast of Lamb with Applemint Stuffing and Bean Bundles (page 153).*

CHRISTMAS PLUM PUDDING ICE-CREAM

Ice-cream

1 cup (250 g/8 oz) white sugar

2 eggs, beaten

1 tablespoon cornflour

2 cups (500 ml/16 fl oz) hot milk

100 g (3½ oz) dark chocolate

2 cups (500 ml/16 fl oz) thickened cream, whipped

3 teaspoons vanilla essence

Filling

2 cups (250 g/8 oz) mixed dried fruits, raisins, currants, sultanas and mixed peel

½ cup (60 g/2 oz) chopped mixed glacé fruit, red and green cherries, apricots and pineapple

¼ cup (60 ml/2 fl oz) rum

¾ cup (90 g/3 oz) slivered almonds, toasted

½ cup (125 ml/4 fl oz) fresh cream

Make the ice-cream: mix the sugar, cornflour and eggs in the top of a double-boiler. Heat the milk and slowly melt the chocolate into it. Slowly add this mixture to the egg mixture, stirring constantly. Stir over hot water until the mixture thickens. Strain and set aside to cool. When cool, fold in the whipped cream and vanilla essence and freeze according to your ice-cream machine's instructions.

Make the filling: combine all the fruit, add the rum, and soak overnight.

Mix together the fruits, almonds, cream and 1 litre (35 fl oz) of the softened chocolate ice-cream.

Pour the mixture into a freezer-proof, bowl-shaped container and freeze until set.

Immerse in hot water to loosen the ice-cream around the edges, and turn out onto a flat serving plate and decorate with holly.

CHRISTMAS CONFECTION CAKE

125 g (4 oz) shelled whole Brazil nuts
125 g (4 oz) shelled whole almonds
125 g (4 oz) shelled walnut halves
¼ cup (60 g/2 oz) chopped dates
2 tablespoons chopped mixed peel
60 g (2 oz) glacé cherries
125 g (4 oz) glacé pineapple, apricots, peaches or pears,
    or a mixture, chopped
¼ cup (60 g/2 oz) sultanas
¼ cup (60 g/2 oz) seeded raisins
⅓ cup (45 g/1½ oz) plain flour
¼ teaspoon baking powder
pinch of salt
⅓ cup (90 g/3 oz) castor sugar
½ teaspoon vanilla essence
2 tablespoons brandy
2 small eggs, beaten

In a large mixing bowl, combine the nuts and fruit. Sift the flour, baking powder and salt and mix with the sugar. Stir into the fruit and nuts. Combine vanilla and brandy with the eggs and stir into fruit and nuts. Mix well. The mixture will be quite stiff. Spoon into a lined and buttered 18-cm (7-in) ring tin or a 22 x 12-cm (8½ x 4½-in) loaf tin and smooth over the top.

Bake in the centre of a 140°C (275°F) oven for 2¼ hours. After the first hour cover with foil, if necessary, to prevent cake from becoming too brown. When cooked, leave to stand in the tin for 10 minutes before turning out to cool on a wire cooling rack. When cold, wrap in aluminium foil and store in the refrigerator.

Cut into small fingers or thin slices to serve with coffee.

MINCE PIES

125 g (4 oz) almonds, blanched and slivered
250 g (8 oz) candied orange peel, chopped
2 Granny Smith apples, cored and chopped
60 g (2 oz) chopped glacé ginger
500 g (16 oz) seedless raisins, halved
500 g (16 oz) currants
500 g (16 oz) sultanas
375 g (12 oz) brown sugar
½ teaspoon each salt, ground nutmeg and mixed spice
grated rind and juice of 1 large lemon
¾ cup (185 ml/6 fl oz) brandy
500 g (16 oz) finely minced beef suet
shortcrust pastry
milk and castor sugar, for glaze

Mix together the nuts, peel and apples. Add the ginger, raisins, currants and sultanas. Stir in the sugar, salt, spices, lemon rind and juice, brandy and suet. Mix thoroughly. This can be kept in dry, tightly covered jars until required.

Roll out enough shortcrust pastry to line 24 small patty pans. Cut lids slightly smaller than the bases. Line each patty pan with pastry. Fill with the fruit mince. Moisten around the edges with water and place pastry lids on top. Glaze with a little milk and sprinkle with castor sugar. Make one or two slits in the top of the pastry.

Bake at 190°C (375°F) for 15 minutes, or until the pastry is golden brown.

Serve with Brandy Butter or Hard Sauce.

Makes 24.

FROSTED GRAPES

2 egg whites
1 kg (2 lb) black grapes
icing sugar, to coat

Whisk the egg whites until stiff. Separate the grapes into small bunches and dip, first into the egg white then into a bowl of sifted icing sugar until coated. Shake gently and place on a wire cooling rack. Put in a warm place to dry overnight.

BRANDY BUTTER OR HARD SAUCE

500 g (16 oz) unsalted butter
500 g (16 oz) icing sugar
8 tablespoons ground almonds
4 tablespoons brandy, or more to taste

Cream together the butter and the icing sugar, add the ground almonds and brandy, and beat well until completely combined.

This amount almost fills a 2.5-litre (4-pint) ice-cream container and will keep for several weeks in an airtight container in the refrigerator.

Serve with Christmas pudding or Mince Pies.

CRYSTALLISED FLOWERS

Some flowers are poisonous, so make sure they are safe before using them.

Australian native flowers to try:

Geraldton wax flower
(*Chamaelaucium uncinatum*)
Wattle (*Acacia* spp.)
Tea tree (*Leptospermum* spp.)
Wax flower (*Eriostemon myoporoides*)
Boronias
Heath myrtle (*Thryptomene* spp.)
Australian fuchsia heath (*Epacris crassifolia*)
Swan River daisy (*Brachycome iberidifolia*)
New South Wales Christmas bush
(*Ceratopetalum gummiferum*)
Astartea spp.
Native fuchsia (*Correa pulchella*)
Kangaroo paw (*Anigozanthos*)
Flannel flower (*Actinotus helianthii*)
Bullock bush (*Templeton refusa*)
Bridal bush *or* wedding bush
(*Ricinocarpus pinifolius*)
Blushing bride (*Serruria florida*)

You will need:

lightly beaten egg white
castor sugar
fresh flowers, well washed and carefully dried

To coat the flowers, use either a paintbrush or dip them carefully by hand in the egg white and then into the sugar, making sure the flowers are completely coated.

Place the flowers on a baking tray lined with greaseproof paper and warm in a very slow oven at 120°C (250°F) for 1 to 1½ hours, or until the flowers are firm and crystallised. Store in an airtight container layered between greaseproof paper. They will keep indefinitely in a cool, dry place.

BOXING DAY
Ideas

In this chapter you will find ideas for cooking new dishes from fresh ingredients as well as using leftovers from the previous days' meals. There is even a recipe for the morning after, included to get you started on Boxing Day! Choose your dishes from the menu on page 160.

BOXING DAY IDEAS

THE MORNING AFTER

SKORDALIA DIP

CREPES (PANCAKES)

HAM AND CHEESE CREPES

POTATOES WITH HAM AND CHEESE

BAKED HAM ROLLS

HAM CREPE CAKE

BOSCAIOLA FOR FETTUCINE

HAM FRITTATA

HAM TARTS

HAM MOUSSE

TURKEY CROQUETTES

TURKEY FRITTATA

TURKEY SALAD

TURKEY CASSEROLE

TURKEY AND VEGETABLE CURRY

VEGETABLE STRUDEL

HAM OR TURKEY WALDORF SALAD

CHRISTMAS TRIFLE

OLD-FASHIONED TRIFLE

RUM AND RAISIN ICE-CREAM

FRUIT PIE WITH RUM SAUCE

SUGGESTED WINES

Dry Crisp White:

Alkoomi West Australian Rhine Riesling

Dry Red:

Penfolds Bin 407 Cabernet Sauvignon

Dessert Wine:

Henschke Noble Rot Rhine Riesling

Boxing Day

In English-speaking countries, Boxing Day was traditionally the day when the rich gave presents to their servants, to the poor, and to the many charitable homes and institutions in the surrounding area. These presents symbolised gifts from God, and the idea originated from the gifts given to the Infant Jesus Christ by the Three Wise Men.

THE MORNING AFTER

300 ml (10 fl oz) orange juice
150 ml (5 fl oz) lemon juice
600 ml (20 fl oz) each dark and white rum
1 small can crushed pineapple
2 tablespoons white sugar
1 tablespoon almond essence
crushed ice
750 ml (24 fl oz) soda water

Combine the orange and lemon juice, rum, pineapple, sugar and almond essence in a large jug or bowl. Add the ice and soda water just before serving.

Makes about 12 glasses.

SKORDALIA DIP

2 cups (500 ml/16 fl oz) mayonnaise
3 cloves garlic, crushed
½ cup (60 g/2 oz) fine breadcrumbs
½ cup (60 g/2 oz) ground almonds
2 tablespoons chopped parsley
salt and pepper

Combine all ingredients, season to taste with salt and pepper, and chill. Serve with vegetable crudités (raw seasonal vegetables).

Serves 12.

CREPES (PANCAKES)

1½ cups (185 g/6 oz) plain flour
½ cup (60 g/2 oz) self-raising flour
½ teaspoon salt
1 cup (250 ml/8 fl oz) evaporated milk
1 cup (250 ml/8 fl oz) water
2 eggs
unsalted butter, for frying

Place all ingredients in a blender and blend until smooth. Add more water if the mixture is too thick. Fry the crepes in a little butter, in a crepe pan or a heavy based frying pan. Stack, interleaved with strips of greaseproof paper. The crepes may be frozen until ready to use. Fill them with your chosen filling, roll up and serve hot.

Serves 6 to 8.

HAM AND CHEESE CREPES

8 thin crepes
4 tablespoons cream cheese
5 tablespoons sour cream
8 tablespoons thickened cream
salt and freshly ground black pepper
8 very thin slices cooked ham
30 g (1 oz) Gruyere cheese, freshly grated

In a mixing bowl, combine the cream cheese with the sour cream and beat them until smoothly blended. Gradually beat in the thickened cream. Add the salt and pepper and chill until ready to serve.

Lay the crepes out flat and spread them evenly with a third of the cream mixture. Cover each crepe with a slice of ham and then spread with half of the remaining cream. Roll up each crepe tightly and arrange side by side in a shallow heatproof dish. Spread with the remaining cream mixture and sprinkle with the Gruyere cheese.

Just before serving, place the crepes under a medium–hot grill for 3 to 4 minutes until the cheese is bubbly.

Serves 4.

POTATOES WITH HAM AND CHEESE

2 very large potatoes
½ cup (125 ml/4 fl oz) sour cream
½ cup (60 g/2 oz) grated tasty cheese
2 spring onions
200 g (6½ oz) cooked ham or bacon, chopped
4–5 button mushrooms, sliced
1 teaspoon wholegrain mustard
extra ¼ cup (30 g/1 oz) grated tasty cheese
¼ teaspoon paprika

Prick the potatoes all over with a fork, place them on an oven rack and bake at 180°C (350°F) for about 1½ hours, or until tender. Halve potatoes and scoop out centre, leaving shell. In a bowl, mash potatoes with sour cream, then stir in cheese, spring onions, ham, mushrooms and mustard. Spoon mixture back into potato skins, top with extra cheese and sprinkle with paprika. Bake for a further 15 minutes, or until the filling is heated and the cheese melted.

Serves 4.

BAKED HAM ROLLS

8 thin slices white bread
butter, for spreading
8 thin slices cooked ham
English mustard
300 ml (10 fl oz) sour cream
black pepper
125 g (4 oz) Cheddar cheese, grated

Spread the slices of bread with butter, place a thin slice of ham on each slice of bread and spread lightly with mustard. Roll up diagonally and arrange in a shallow, buttered ovenproof dish. Pour the sour cream over, sprinkle with freshly ground black pepper and grated cheese. Bake at 180°C (350°F) for 40 minutes.

Serves 8.

PREVIOUS PAGE: *Clockwise from the left: poppadums, cold Glazed Ham with Cherries (page 92), Turkey Casserole (page 166), Potatoes with Ham and Cheese, Ham Crepe Cake, Ham Mousse and Turkey and Vegetable Curry (page 168).*

HAM CREPE CAKE

8–10 crepes or pancakes
500 g (16 oz) ham, sliced paper thin
butter
1 tablespoon Parmesan cheese
185 g (6 oz) butter
⅓ cup (90 g/3 oz) capers
½ cup (125 g/4 oz) finely chopped pickled gherkins
1 lemon, finely chopped, skin and all
cayenne pepper

Assemble the cake by placing alternate layers of crepes and ham on a greased baking dish, finishing with a crepe. Dot with small knobs of butter, sprinkle with Parmesan cheese and bake at 180°C (350°F) for 30 to 35 minutes, or until thoroughly heated through. Make sure the edges do not dry out. If they do, lower the heat and cover with aluminium foil or greaseproof paper. Place the remaining ingredients for the sauce in a heavy based saucepan and continually stir over a low heat until the butter heats through and becomes creamy. Serve the sauce separately in a warm jug. Serve cut into wedges and pour the sauce over.

Serves 6 to 8.

BOSCAIOLA FOR FETTUCCINE

10–12 button mushrooms, sliced
20 g (⅔ oz) butter
1 clove garlic, crushed
4 slices cooked ham, chopped
salt and pepper
300 ml (10 fl oz) fresh cream
1 tablespoon chopped parsley
Parmesan cheese, grated for serving
fettuccine for 4

Gently fry mushrooms in the butter. Add the garlic, ham, salt and pepper and stir until hot. Add cream and parsley and heat through. Pour over hot, freshly cooked fettuccine and toss well. Serve with the Parmesan cheese.

Serves 4.

HAM FRITTATA

45 g (1½ oz) butter
2 small onions, finely chopped
1 red sweet pepper (capsicum), sliced
1 green sweet pepper (capsicum), sliced
3–4 small zucchini, sliced
6 eggs
½ cup (125 ml/4 fl oz) cream
extra 30 g (1 oz) butter
125 g (4 oz) cooked ham, diced
125 g (4 oz) Cheddar cheese, grated

Melt the butter in a large frying pan and gently fry the onions, peppers and zucchini. Beat together the eggs and cream. Add the extra butter to the pan, pour in the egg mixture, add the vegetables and ham and stir lightly over a low heat for about 10 minutes, or until it is firm underneath. Sprinkle the cheese over and place it under a hot grill until the cheese melts. Cut into wedges and serve warm.

Serves 6 to 8.

HAM TARTS

500 g (16 oz) shortcrust or puff pastry
125 g (4 oz) cooked ham, diced
1 tablespoon mayonnaise
1 tablespoon French mustard
pinch of paprika
150 ml (5 fl oz) thickened cream
chopped parsley

Roll out the pastry of your choice on a lightly floured board and line 6 to 8 individual flan tins or one large flan tin. Bake blind at 180°C (350°F) for 12 to 15 minutes. Cool. Combine the diced ham with the mayonnaise, mustard and paprika. Whip the cream and fold it into the mixture. Pour the mixture into the pie shells and sprinkle with the chopped parsley and a little paprika. Bake at 180°C (350°F) until the centre is firm and golden.

Serves 6 to 8.

HAM MOUSSE

3 egg yolks
2 cups (500 ml/16 fl oz) milk
1½ tablespoons powdered gelatine
½ cup (125 ml/4 fl oz) chicken stock or hot water
2 cups (500 g/16 oz) chopped ham
salt and white pepper to taste
¼ cup (60 ml/2 fl oz) fresh cream, whipped

In the top of a double boiler, whisk together the egg yolks and milk over gently boiling water, stirring continuously until the mixture is smooth and thick. Dissolve the gelatine in the stock or in the hot water and stir it into the egg mixture. Allow to cool then add the chopped ham and salt and pepper. Pour the mixture into a mixing bowl. Cover and chill until nearly set. Fold in the whipped cream. Pour into an oiled mould, cover, and allow to set in the refrigerator overnight. Turn out onto a flat plate to serve.

Serves 6 to 8.

TURKEY CROQUETTES

cooked turkey, minced
1–2 onions, finely chopped
fresh white breadcrumbs
1 egg, lightly beaten
extra breadcrumbs, for coating
oil, for deep frying

Combine the turkey meat and the onions with the breadcrumbs. Bind the mixture with the beaten egg. Add salt and pepper. Shape into small balls or cylinders and roll them in the extra breadcrumbs until completely coated. Heat the oil in a deep fryer and cook the croquettes until golden brown and crisp.

Serves 6 to 8.

TURKEY FRITTATA

1 large red or yellow sweet pepper (capsicum)
1 small packet frozen spinach
1 large potato
10 eggs
6 tablespoons grated Parmesan cheese
salt and freshly ground black pepper to taste
2 cups (500 g/16 oz) cooked turkey meat, diced
¼ cup (60 g/2 oz) chopped parsley
4 sun-dried tomatoes, chopped
butter, for frying

Cut the sweet pepper in half, remove the seeds and roast it at 220°C (425°F) for about 20 to 30 minutes, until the skin blisters. Cool, peel off the skin, and cut into strips. Thaw the spinach and drain well. Boil the potato, cool, peel, and cut into cubes. Beat the eggs well, add the Parmesan, salt and pepper, and the remaining ingredients. Melt the butter in a heavy based 24 cm (10½ in) frying pan. Pour in the egg mixture and cook over a low heat until nearly set. Brown under a hot grill. Serve in wedges.

Serves 8 to 12.

TURKEY SALAD

2 cups (500 g/16 oz) cooked turkey meat, diced
⅔ cup 180 g/ 6 oz) dill pickles, sliced
1 red onion, sliced into rings
1 cup (250 g/8 oz) black olives, pitted
1 55-g (2-oz) tin anchovy fillets, optional

Dressing
2 teaspoons Dijon mustard
1 tablespoon coarsely chopped tarragon
1 tablespoon cider or white wine vinegar
3 tablespoons olive oil
freshly ground black pepper

Shake all the dressing ingredients together in a screw-top jar. Place all salad ingredients into a serving bowl. Fold the dressing through the salad.

Serves 4 to 6.

TURKEY CASSEROLE

2 egg yolks
150 ml (5 fl oz) milk
salt and pepper
1 small can tomato purée
1 large onion, chopped
500 g (16 oz) cooked turkey meat, chopped
   into cubes
15 g (½ oz) plain flour
½ teaspoon ground thyme
4 tablespoons turkey stock or water
15 g (½ oz) butter
salt and pepper to taste
4 large tomatoes, peeled and sliced
60 g (2 oz) tasty cheese, grated

In the top of a double boiler, whisk the egg yolks and the milk together and cook them slowly over gently boiling water until the custard is smooth and thick. Add the salt and pepper and allow the mixture to cool. In a covered pan, sauté the onion in butter until it is soft but not brown. Add the chopped turkey meat and stir in the flour. Add the tomato purée, stock, salt and pepper and thyme and gently cook for several minutes.

Place the mixture in an ovenproof dish. Cover with a layer of sliced tomatoes. Pour the custard mixture over and sprinkle the top with the grated cheese. Bake at 180°C (350°F) for 30 minutes, or until the cheese is golden brown.

Serves 4.

> *Turkey casserole is the perfect recipe to use up some of the inevitable turkey leftovers. If you find you still have meat leftover, don't forget the humble sandwich. There's nothing like sitting down to a snack of homemade sandwiches on a lazy holiday afternoon.*

RIGHT: *Turkey Casserole.*

TURKEY AND VEGETABLE CURRY

8 tablespoons sunflower oil
1 large onion, chopped
1 teaspoon Tabasco sauce
2 cloves garlic, crushed
1 tablespoon ground ginger
1 tablespoon ground turmeric
1 teaspoon ground cumin
1 teaspoon garam masala
pinch of salt
400-g (13-oz) can tomatoes, chopped
1 kg (2 lb) cooked turkey meat, diced
100 g (3½ oz) green beans, topped and tailed
100 g (3½ oz) cauliflower florets
¼ cup (60 ml/2 fl oz) chicken stock
3 tablespoons chopped coriander

Heat the oil in a heavy based pan and fry the onion, Tabasco and garlic for 5 minutes, until softened but not brown. Add the spices and salt, and stir-fry for 1 minute. Add the tomatoes and diced turkey and cook gently for about 5 minutes. Add the remaining ingredients and continue cooking for a further 5 to 10 minutes, stirring occasionally.

Serve with rice, poppadums and a selection of chutneys.

Serves 6 to 12.

VEGETABLE STRUDEL

6 sheets filo pastry
½ cup (125 g/4 oz) finely chopped leeks
½ cup (125 g/4 oz) chopped red sweet
   pepper (capsicum)
100 g (3½ oz) mushrooms, chopped
1 stick celery, chopped
1 carrot, grated
2 tablespoons chopped parsley
1 cup (250 g/8 oz) cottage cheese
1 cup (250 g/ 8 oz) grated Parmesan cheese
1 egg, beaten
¼ cup (15 g/½ oz) fresh white breadcrumbs

Basil Sauce
15 g (½ oz) butter
1 clove garlic, crushed
1 tablespoon plain flour
¾ cup (185 ml/6 fl oz) milk
½ cup (125 ml/4 fl oz) fresh cream
2½ tablespoons chopped basil
1 tablespoon grated Parmesan cheese

Lay out a sheet of filo and brush it with melted butter, place another piece of pastry on top, brush with butter and repeat until all pastry is layered. Sauté all vegetables in remaining butter until tender, for about 10 minutes. Drain, cool, and mix with parsley, cheeses, egg and breadcrumbs.

Place the filling on the shorter end of the pastry rectangle, leaving about 2 cm (¾ in) each side. Fold pastry over filling then fold sides over filling and roll up like a Swiss roll. Brush with melted butter and place on a baking tray. Bake at 200°C (400°F) for 20 to 25 minutes, or until golden brown. Allow to stand for 5 minutes before serving with basil sauce.

Make the basil sauce: melt the butter with the garlic in a saucepan, stir in the flour for 1 minute. Remove from the heat, add the milk and cream, and cook for about 2 minutes, stirring continuously, until mixture boils. Stir in the basil and cheese. Pour over the Vegetable Strudel just before serving.

Serves 6 to 8.

HAM OR TURKEY WALDORF SALAD

Salad

1 crisp Iceberg lettuce

1 tablespoon chopped walnuts

1 green apple, cored and chopped

2 tablespoons chopped parsley

2 tablespoons cooked ham or turkey meat, chopped

1 cup (125 g/4 oz) watercress sprigs

Dressing

juice of 1 lemon

3 tablespoons olive oil

½ cup (125 ml/4 fl oz) thickened or sour cream

salt and pepper to taste

Tear the lettuce into a serving bowl. Sprinkle the walnuts, apple, parsley and ham or turkey over the lettuce.

Make the dressing: whisk all ingredients together until creamy. Pour the dressing over the salad and sprinkle watercress sprigs on top.

Serves 6 to 8.

RUM AND RAISIN ICE-CREAM

1 cup (250 g/8 oz) seedless raisins

1 litre (35 fl oz) fresh cream

8 egg yolks

1 cup (250 g/8 oz) castor sugar

¼ cup (60 ml/2 fl oz) rum

Soak the raisins in boiling water to cover for 1 hour. Drain well and place in a small bowl. In the top of a double boiler, combine half the cream with the egg yolks and sugar. Stir continuously over gently boiling water until the mixture starts to thicken. Remove from the heat and stir in the remaining cream and rum. Cool, then chill in the refrigerator for 1 hour. When cold, mix in an ice-cream churn for 20 to 30 minutes. Stop the churn and carefully stir in the raisins. Complete churning as directed for your machine and freeze.

Serves 12.

FRUIT PIE WITH RUM SAUCE

100 g (3½ oz) brown sugar

¼ teaspoon salt

30 g (1 oz) plain flour

2 bananas, peeled and sliced

2 large ripe pears, cored, peeled and sliced

2 large slices pineapple, peeled, cored and chopped

5 dried figs, chopped

juice of 1 lemon

275 g (9 oz) shortcrust pastry

milk or beaten egg, to glaze

Rum Sauce

4 tablespoons brown sugar

2 teaspoons arrowroot or cornflour

½ teaspoon ground cinnamon

6 tablespoons rum

8 tablespoons orange or pineapple juice

Sift the brown sugar, salt and flour together into a mixing bowl. Add the prepared fruit and mix carefully until all the fruit is well coated with the mixture. Add the lemon juice and mix well.

Roll half the pastry out to a round shape and use it to line a 22-cm (8½-in) flan dish or tin. Fill with the fruit mixture, adding any remaining juices. Roll out the remaining pastry and cover the filling, sealing at the edges of the pie. Make several slits in the top of the pastry and brush with milk or lightly beaten egg. Bake at 200°C (400°F) for 25 to 30 minutes, until golden brown. Serve warm with the rum sauce.

Make the rum sauce: combine the sugar, arrowroot and cinnamon in a small saucepan. Gradually blend in all the liquids. Cook slowly, stirring continuously, until the sauce begins to thicken. Bring to the boil and simmer for 1 minute. Pour into a jug and serve with the Fruit Pie.

Serves 8 to 12.

CHRISTMAS TRIFLE

½ plain sponge cake
60 ml (2 fl oz) Madeira or sherry
6 macaroons
60 g (2 oz) raspberry jam or 1 punnet fresh raspberries
thick pastry cream (see recipe instructions)
1 cup (250 ml/8 fl oz) fresh cream
¼ cup (60 g/2 oz) slivered almonds
6 crystallised flowers, pansies or violets

Pastry Cream
700 ml (22 fl oz) milk
4 egg yolks
5 tablespoons castor sugar
6 tablespoons plain flour
1 teaspoon cornflour

Cut the sponge cake into 10-cm (4-in) squares and place it in a glass serving bowl. Pour over the Madeira or sherry. Break the macaroons into pieces and sprinkle them over the top. Allow to stand for 15 minutes, so the sponge cake absorbs the Madeira or sherry.

Meanwhile, make the pastry cream: heat the milk, mix the egg yolks, sugar and flours together, add the hot milk and whisk the mixture until smooth. Place the mixture in a saucepan and cook, whisking constantly until thick and smooth. Cover and cool.

Spoon the raspberry jam over the sponge and macaroons after they have been standing for 15 minutes. Pour the pastry cream over the trifle. Whip the cream until it is thick and spread it over the pastry cream. Garnish the trifle with the almonds and crystallised fruit.

Serves 8 to 12.

OLD-FASHIONED TRIFLE

500 ml (16 fl oz) port wine jelly
250 g (8 oz) Savoyardi biscuits or sponge fingers
250 g (8 oz) cherry jam
250 ml (8 fl oz) sherry
100 ml (3½ fl oz) brandy
1 small can or jar pitted sweet or sour cherries, drained
600 ml (20 fl oz) fresh cream, whipped
maraschino cherries and nuts, to decorate

Vanilla Custard
5 egg yolks
100 g (3½ oz) white sugar
25 g (1 oz) cornflour
1 teaspoon vanilla flavouring essence
600 ml (20 fl oz) milk

Make the port wine jelly according to the instructions on the packet. Cool until it begins to set. Spread the Savoyardi biscuits or sponge fingers with cherry jam and place them in the bottom of a glass bowl. Sprinkle with sherry and brandy and leave them to absorb the jam and the sherry or brandy.

Meanwhile, make the vanilla custard: beat the egg yolks, sugar, cornflour and vanilla together. Pour the hot milk in and stir well. Place the mixture in a saucepan and bring to the boil, stirring constantly, then set aside to cool.

Pour the custard over the sponge fingers and refrigerate until set. Sprinkle with drained cherries and then pour the cold jelly over. Cover and refrigerate overnight. Top the trifle with whipped cream and decorate with cherries and nuts before serving.

Serves 12.

PREVIOUS PAGE: *Old-fashioned Trifle and Rum and Raisin Ice-cream (page 169).*

CHRISTMAS HOLIDAYS

BY MYRON LYSENKO

During the Christmas holidays
people want to celebrate,
want to be happy,
want to be with friends and relatives,
want to over-eat and over-drink
and over-do the merriment.
They outdo themselves,
trying to buy the most frivolous present.
They shop until they drop.
They give me Christmas cards
when they know I really want vanilla slices.
Merry Christmas to you
Merry Christmas to you
Merry Christmas to everybody;
Merry Christmas to you.
All I want to do at Christmas
is to watch my regular television programs
and spend days of minimum movement
watching the test cricket;
lying out of the sun,
keeping cool enough for comfort
and reading the weekend papers
all week long.
Merry Christmas to you
Merry Christmas to you
Merry Christmas to everybody;
Merry Christmas to you.

INDEX